QUEEN AND COUNTRY

THE FIFTY-YEAR REIGN OF ELIZABETH II

WILLIAM SHAWCROSS

Simon & Schuster
New York London Toronto Sydney Singapore

For Ellie, with my love

L

SIMON & SCHUSTER
Rockefeller Center
1230 Avenue of the Americas
New York, NY 10020

First published by BBC Worldwide Limited,
Woodlands, 80 Wood Lane, London W12 0TT, 2002

For information about special discounts for bulk purchases,
please contact Simon & Schuster Special Sales:
1-800-456-6798 or business@simonandschuster.com.

Manufactured in France

10 9 8 7 6 5 4 3 2 1

Library of Congress Cataloging-in-Publication Data
is available.

ISBN 0-7432-2676-3

BBC Worldwide would like to thank the following for providing
photographs and for permission to reproduce copyright material.
While every effort has been made to trace and acknowledge all
copyright holders, we would like to apologise should there have
been any errors or omissions.

Assignments Photographers/Corbis page 175 (Bryn Colton);
Associated Press 53; BBC 153, 154; Bettman/Corbis 124; Camera
Press 2 (Snowdon), 6, 9, 10, 15, 17 (Tom Blau), 20, 22, 28, 30, 32,
34 (Bassano), 35 (Marcus Adams), 42 (Beaton), 51, 60, 68, 73l
(Dave Waterman), 73r (Peter Abbey), 80, 81, 94, 95, 105 (Penny
Tweedie), 112, 116, 129, 140 (Lichfield), 149 (Roger Garwood), 157
(A Edwards), 166 (John Shelley), 168, 170 (Godfrey Argent), 213,
220 (R S Martin), 223 (Geoff Howard), 231t, 231b (Stewart Mark);
Lionel Cherruault 150; Tim Graham 64, 207; Hulton-Deutsch
Collection/Corbis 87, 102, 179; Hulton Getty 26, 29, 37t, 46, 114;
Press Association 12, 37b, 39, 40, 47, 54, 55, 56l, 56r, 58, 69, 82,
98t, 98b, 100, 109, 115, 118, 131, 134, 144, 162, 164, 187, 209, 217,
219, 226, 232, 237; Popperfoto 31, 79, 90, 120, 160, 233; David
Secombe 183, 190, 195, 202; Sport & General 181; Topham 62,
67, 71, 127, 174 (Peter Kemp), 180, 180r, 196, 198.

Every effort has been made to trace copyright holders of material
included in this book. However, the Publishers would like to
apologize for any errors or omissions and invite the relevant
parties to contact them with details.

Contents

Death and Devotion

Early in the morning of Sunday, 31 August 1997, Diana, Princess of Wales, was killed in a car crash in Paris. The brutal destruction of such a beautiful, young and celebrated Princess was greeted with horror.

A few hours after her death, the Prime Minister Tony Blair appeared on television to hail her as 'The People's Princess'. For the next week television covered almost nothing but the death of the Princess and the impact upon the royal family – and in particular on her two young sons. The nation, or at least a visible and vocal part of it, appeared to be consumed by grief. Tens of thousands of people made pilgrimages to her home at Kensington Palace, London, and left bunches of flowers wrapped in cellophane, toys, notes and poems. Others journeyed to Althorp, her family's stately home in Northamptonshire.

This was not quite mass hysteria, but it was a massive display of group emotion of a kind that had never been seen before in Britain. Many older people, schooled in a time when emotions were more strictly controlled, both in public and private, found themselves surprised or even alienated by the spectacle. But the Princess had been a celebrity of the modern age, much admired by millions. To them her death was not just a shock, but a source of bereavement. Many of those who did not share the intensity of this pain felt excluded.

Widespread sympathy was extended to her family, especially to her two young sons, William and Harry. They and their father, Prince Charles, from whom Diana was divorced, were staying at Balmoral, the Queen's summer home in Scotland, when Diana died. Within hours of hearing of her death, Prince Charles flew to Paris to escort the body home. He then returned to his family at Balmoral. Word came from Buckingham Palace that the Queen was

◁ The funeral of Diana, Princess of Wales at Westminster Abbey on 6 September 1997.

anxious above all to comfort and protect her grandsons. Such a decision was hardly improper but, as the expressions of popular grief grew during the week after Diana's death, so did the expressions of outrage at the inaccessibility of the Queen and her family.

The crowds outside Kensington Palace and Buckingham Palace grew larger and, the media reported, in some cases more resentful. Why was the Queen not back in London? Why was she not showing her own anguish and sharing that of her subjects? Such aggressive questions were repeated, exaggerated and headlined by television and tabloid journalists. 'SHOW US YOU CARE' demanded one tabloid of the Queen. Others castigated and blamed Prince Charles.

On Friday, the day before the funeral, Prince Charles and his two sons returned to London and walked amongst the huge stacks of flowers and the people milling around Kensington Palace. Princes William and Harry behaved with impeccable courage, and all three were warmly received. The Queen flew down from Scotland. As she drove up to the Victoria Memorial by the gates of Buckingham Palace, she stopped her car and, with Prince Philip, got out to look at the tributes and speak to the people gathered there. She did not know what to expect from the crowd; some of her aides feared hostility. But when the Queen began to talk, the crowd responded not with anger but with politeness, even relief.

She then walked through the Palace gates and shortly afterwards paid a live television tribute to Diana. Through the window behind her you could see the crowds milling around the Victoria Memorial. The Queen, who never likes to display emotion in public, spoke of her admiration for her late daughter-in-law, for whom public emotion was very important.

That night tens of thousands of people slept in the streets to guarantee a good view of the funeral procession. There had been discussions all week about the route and the nature of the funeral; in the end the organization was flawless. On a beautiful sunny September morning, the cortège carried the Princess's body from Kensington Palace to Westminster Abbey. The service was broadcast on a large screen in Parliament Square and transmitted around the world. Diana's brother Charles Spencer gave the eulogy, which was applauded in the Square outside. Elton John, a friend of the Princess, sang to her, and the Prime Minister

The Queen and Prince Philip in front of the gates of Buckingham Palace, looking at tributes to Diana, Princess of Wales on the day before her funeral.

read the lesson. The Princess's body was then taken by road to Althorp, where it was buried on an island in an artificial lake.

The events of this extraordinary week were powerful and disturbing. Some people said it would change the monarchy for ever; others seized the week for the republican cause. But it was hard for anyone to say that the week showed that the monarchy was irrelevant to the people of Britain.

Amongst the many images of the week, one that I found most arresting was of the Queen two days before the funeral, looking at the mass of flowers that had been laid outside Crathie Church near Balmoral. She was all in black and bending over to read the words inscribed on the cards. She turned to find herself being observed by the world through the lenses of many cameras, and turned away again. It reminded me of the photograph taken 45 years earlier when she, her mother and her grandmother stood all in black near the coffin of her father, King George VI. Then she had been Queen for only a few days; now she was in the forty-sixth year of her reign. Then the cameras had been distant and almost respectful; now they were invasive.

I thought how lonely she must feel, and how perplexed she must be by the vast changes through which Britain has passed in the decades since her accession. In this book I have attempted to explain some of these changes and her responses to them. I have drawn especially on interviews given for the accompanying television series *Queen and Country*. Her story, I believe, is one of duty done with devotion and diligence in a kingdom that has been utterly transformed around her.

one

The African Queen

It has become a cliché to say that a monarchy needs magic. A republic needs no enchantment and rarely possesses it. Monarchy requires sentiment, belief and imagination.

There was something magical about this Queen's accession to the throne. She is the only woman known to have gone up a tree a Princess and come down a Queen.

By the middle of 1951 her father, King George VI, was seriously ill with cancer, though thanks to his doctors' reticence, he and his family thought he merely had bronchial troubles. In September 1951 surgeons removed his left lung, and he was forced to cancel a visit to Australia and New Zealand in early 1952. He and the government decided that his heir, Princess Elizabeth, and her young husband, Prince Philip, should make the voyage instead. They had just completed a successful trip to Canada, which Prince Philip remembered long afterwards as one of the most interesting they took together.

The 25-year-old Princess and her husband left on the morning of 31 January 1952. Her parents came with the Prime Minister, Winston Churchill, and other officials to see them off at London airport. Photographs show the King without a hat, the winter wind blowing through his hair, his face gaunt, even pained. He waved his daughter goodbye as the Argonaut *Atalanta* sped along the runway and into the air.

The British Overseas Airways Corporation (BOAC) had taken several rows of seats out of the back of the plane to make a small cabin for the royal couple. Amongst the party on this tour were courtiers and servants who had played an important part in the Princess's life. There was Bobo MacDonald, who had been with her since childhood. Bobo was a Scotswoman who was able to combine

◁ In February 1952, Princess Elizabeth and Prince Philip arrived in Nairobi, the first stop on what they expected to be a long Commonwealth tour.

Princess Elizabeth's father, George VI, her mother and her sister waved goodbye to the royal couple on the tarmac at London airport. It was the last time the King was to see his elder daughter.

loyalty and discretion with frankness sometimes bordering on fierceness. She had arrived as a nursemaid when Princess Elizabeth was a small child; she shared a room with the young Princess for many years and remained her dresser and unofficial adviser until her death in 1993.

There was Martin Charteris who had been appointed her Assistant Private Secretary in 1950. A lighthearted soul who loved to laugh uproariously, he had served in the King's Royal Rifle Corps during the war. In 1946 he became the

Head of Military Intelligence in Palestine and greatly impressed Chaim Weizman, the Zionist leader and first President of Israel. Charteris said to me once that he fell in love with the Queen the first time he met her and that it lasted for ever. He remained with the Queen for most of the next three decades, becoming her Private Secretary from 1972 until his retirement in 1977. Witty and wise, he was always amongst the most delightful members of the household.

Lieutenant Michael Parker was equerry-in-waiting to the Prince and Princess, and was the Prince's Private Secretary. Mike Parker had been a good friend of Prince Philip since their time together in the navy. He was a funny and out-spoken Australian whose open character chimed with that of the Prince; the Princess also found it easy to relax with him. Lady Pamela Mountbatten, the outgoing daughter of Lord Louis Mountbatten, a cousin of both the Prince and Princess, was also on the tour. Lady Pamela had been bridesmaid to Princess Elizabeth in 1947. Continuing the Mountbatten tradition, set by her grandfather and father, of accompanying the heir to the throne on a royal tour, she was lady-in-waiting to the Princess for this long trip.

There was a holiday atmosphere on board the plane – they were all happy to escape the British winter for the sun and exotic travel, even if much of the tour was due to be formal and arduous. First stop was Kenya, where the colonial government had built the Prince and Princess a house in the Aberdare Mountains called Sagana Lodge, as a present to mark their wedding. After a few days' work and holiday in Kenya they would embark in SS *Gothic* at Mombasa to sail to Ceylon and then Australia and New Zealand.

Late in the day, the Argonaut had to touch down at the RAF base of El-Adem in Libya to refuel. The crew changed and the new pilot was Captain Ronald Ballantine, a tall man with the elegant moustache favoured in those days by airmen. He remembers above all the fun of the flight south. They flew across north-east Africa, and the royal couple asked Ballantine to circle Kilimanjaro so that they could take photographs. The captain obliged, though he was nervous that it would prevent him from touching down on schedule. As they descended towards Nairobi, the Princess asked if they could come into the cockpit and stand behind the pilot to watch the approach and landing. It was against all the rules, even in that era of few rules, but he agreed and all went well. They landed precisely on time; Ballantine was happy.

The Princess and her husband went straight to Nairobi for official engagements. Then they drove to take possession of their gift, Sagana Lodge, where they had time to fish and walk and shoot cine-film, one of their enthusiasms. On the afternoon of 5 February, the royal couple were taken from there to Treetops, which was, as its name suggests, a treehouse. It was an enticingly simple shack in a large fig tree, overlooking a salt lick and pool to which elephants, rhinos, deer and other animals came at night.

However, there were dangers. This area was controlled by the Mau Mau rebels whose insurgency would soon tear colonial Kenya apart. Later, they burned down Treetops. There were animal threats as well. As the Prince and Princess and their party walked through the trees towards the fig tree in the afternoon sun, they saw under it a cow elephant and two calves. They debated whether they should be sensible and quietly withdraw or whether they should walk towards the elephant and risk frightening her. The Prince and Princess wanted to carry on, and they did so, across the grass, up the ladder and into the treehouse.

The evening was perfection. Monkeys had got into the rooms and festooned the branches with rolls of lavatory paper. The Princess spent the evening filming as much as she could. Pamela Mountbatten recollects, 'There were a lot of antics in the salt lick, the elephants blowing salt all over themselves and all over the monkeys and pigeons. It was a real sort of clown turn and great fun.'

After a brief sleep, Mike Parker persuaded the Princess to climb up a ladder from the main cabin to another platform 30 feet above. There, right on top of the tree, they watched the sunrise over the mountains. Parker remembered ever after that as they sat there a large white eagle circled and swooped low above their heads. He was concerned it might even dive on them. Later he realized that the appearance of the eagle had almost exactly coincided with the moment when the King died.

The previous day at Sandringham, his Norfolk country house, the 56-year-old King was feeling better and had spent many happy hours shooting rabbits. He went

Treetops was an enchanting hut in a fig tree, overlooking a salt lick where wild animals gathered every evening.

to bed as normal, but he died in the night when a blood clot reached his heart. His valet found his body when he came to draw the curtains at 7.30 a.m. on 6 February.

Edward Ford, Assistant Private Secretary to the King, was in London and remembers, 'At about a quarter to nine I suddenly got a telephone call from Sandringham, from Sir Alan Lascelles, the King's Private Secretary, who just said, "Edward, Hyde Park Corner. Go and tell the Prime Minister and Queen Mary" and he rang off.' Hyde Park Corner was Palace code for 'The King has died'.

Ford drove himself straight to 10 Downing Street to inform the Prime Minister. He was sent up to Winston Churchill's bedroom and found him still in bed writing, the covers strewn with papers. By the bed flickered a green candle for relighting his cigar.

'Prime Minister, I have bad news for you,' said Ford. 'The King has died. I know no details.' 'Bad news?' said Churchill. 'The worst.' Britain's war and peacetime leader pushed aside the papers. 'How unimportant these matters seem now.' He telephoned his Foreign Secretary, Anthony Eden, but because they could not scramble the line they talked in code. 'Our big chief has gone – we must have a Cabinet.'

Contact with Kenya in those days was not easy; the coded message – Hyde Park Corner – was delayed. The young Queen had returned to Sagana Lodge, tired but exhilarated, and was looking forward to another day in the African bush.

Martin Charteris heard the news first. He was staying a few miles away from the lodge, at the Outspan Hotel, with the journalists who were covering the royal tour. Just after 2 p.m. Granville Roberts, a journalist for the *East African Standard*, rushed to tell Charteris that Reuters had sent a flash from London saying that the King had died. Charteris immediately called Mike Parker at the lodge and said, 'I have a rumour from the press corps that our employer's father has died.' Parker says he replied, 'I cannot react to a rumour. Please confirm or deny when sure.' Parker was in a little office next to the Queen's sitting room where she was writing letters. The joining door was open. He closed it, switched on a short wave radio on the desk, and turned on the BBC very low. 'I heard bells and then a repeated announcement by John Snagge that the King had died.' He switched off the radio and walked round the outside of the lodge to Prince Philip's bedroom. The Prince was asleep; Parker woke him and told him the news. 'This will be the most appalling shock,' said the Prince. Parker later commented, 'He looked as if I'd dropped half the world on him. I never felt so sorry for anyone in my life.' The Prince then went to his wife and asked her to come with him into the garden.

From the window Parker and Pamela Mountbatten could see the couple walking up and down the lawn, with Philip talking and talking while they both tried to come to terms with the enormity of what had happened. The Princess had lost her beloved father and become monarch in one second.

A very shocked new Queen came back into the lodge. Pamela Mountbatten forgot that she should curtsy, rushed to hug her and said, 'I'm so sorry.'

The Queen replied, 'Oh, thank you. But I'm so sorry, it means we all have to go back to England and it's upsetting everyone's plans.' Only at that moment, said Pamela, did she fully realize the enormity of it all – that it was the King, not just this young woman's father, who had died.

By now Martin Charteris had arrived from the Outspan Hotel to assist 'the lady we must now call Queen'. 'I'm a romantic,' he said, 'and I think she seized her destiny with both hands. I asked her what she wanted to be called and she replied, "Elizabeth, of course".' Charteris had been carrying a file of accession papers with him ever since the trip to Canada, in case the King died while they were away. Accession is immediate – 'The King is dead. Long live the King' is an ancient cry.

The death of George VI, aged only 56, was a great shock to the British people.

With Charteris, the new Queen drafted telegrams to Churchill, and to Ceylon, Australia and New Zealand, cancelling the rest of the tour. She was totally composed, keeping her feelings tight inside. All those present were astounded by her calmness. Pamela Mountbatten and Bobo Macdonald, both far less calm, flung things into suitcases. They were helped by Kathini Graham, an official at Government House, who had come up from Nairobi. Most of the luggage had been sent straight to the *Gothic*. 'By dint of opening quite a few suitcases, we found black shoes and a black coat. The only thing we didn't find was a hat,' said Graham. One of the first official telegrams of the new reign was to order a black hat to be delivered on their return to London airport.

Mike Parker organized the journey. He learned that the Argonaut and crew that had flown them out were still in Mombasa. Captain Ballantine was called from a swim in the sea to hear the news, and was told to get straight back to his plane. Rather than bring the Queen south to Mombasa, Ballantine was told to pick her up in Entebbe, several hundred miles closer to London. A Dakota DC-3, the redoubtable workhorse of World War II, was found in Nairobi. Parker commandeered the plane, and it was flown up to the airstrip at Nanyuki, a few miles from Sagana Lodge, which the Queen's party left at around 5 p.m. The Queen said goodbye to all those working at the lodge; the Kenyan chauffeur knelt to kiss her shoes. Since she was not in proper mourning attire, Martin Charteris asked the press to take no photographs. They agreed; as the official party drove out of the lodge, they were treated to what would now be the extraordinary sight of newsmen with their large box cameras lying at their feet.

It was still only a couple of hours after the Queen had heard the news, but it had already spread across what might well be called the bush telegraph. Groups of villagers came out and stood silently by the road, their heads bowed, as the royal entourage passed by. They were murmuring 'Shauri mbya kabisa' – 'The very worst has happened.'

At Nanyuki, the pilot was anxious to take off because he had to fly over the Aberdares, where a violent storm was clearly gathering. But the new Queen stood for a long moment looking out of the door of the plane at the African bush she was leaving, before turning and taking her seat. The plane bucked over the mountains just as the storm closed in. When they landed in Entebbe the weather was so bad that Captain Ballantine, who had already arrived from Mombasa, felt he had to delay. London was constantly trying to contact him through the control tower, urging him to leave, but 'I wasn't taking any chances. I had a Queen now, not a Princess… I couldn't possibly take off down the runway into the gloom and turbulence over the lake.' The Queen and Prince Philip had to spend two hours in the departure lounge, making small talk with the Governor of Uganda, Sir Andrew Cohen, and his wife. 'The Queen,' said Pamela Mountbatten, 'was absolute perfection, you know, not a tremor – icy self-control but agony inside obviously.'

Finally, Ballantine thought that the storm had lifted enough for him to take off, and the plane rushed down the runway and into the stormy sky over the darkness of Lake Victoria. The Queen and Prince Philip went straight to the cabin at the back of the plane and, says Pamela Mountbatten, 'one hopes that at that point she had her howl'.

The British monarchy is the oldest in Europe; indeed, it is the oldest European institution of any kind save the Papacy. Queen Elizabeth II can trace her descent directly from Egbert, King of England from 827 to 839. The great-great-grandchild of Queen Victoria, she had now become the fortieth monarch since William the Conqueror seized the crown of England in 1066.

The basis for succession was defined in the constitutional struggles of the seventeenth century, fought between those who believed in the divine right of kings – that the sovereign was responsible to God alone – and Parliament, which believed that the sovereign's title rested upon the willingness to rule within the law and through Parliament. Parliament prevailed: the Act of Settlement of 1701 established that the sovereign rules under law. Indeed, its full title was 'An Act for the further limitation of the Crown and better securing the rights and liberties of the subject'. It was one of the changes vital to the creation of a modern constitutional monarchy.

The Duke and Duchess of York holding Princess Elizabeth, soon after her birth in 1926. At that time the Duke did not expect to become King.

Elizabeth was born not to be Queen, but to be the niece of the future King. Her father, Prince Albert, Duke of York, the second son of King George V, was a shy man with a crippling stammer who had hoped to live his life in the shadow of the throne rather than upon it. His elder brother David was due to inherit. In 1923 Albert married a young Scottish aristocrat, Elizabeth Bowes-Lyon, who became one of the most popular members of the royal family in the twentieth century. Their children, Elizabeth and Margaret Rose, were born in 1926 and 1930.

For the first 10 years of her life, Princess Elizabeth Alexandra Mary had an undemanding and happy childhood, spent at 145 Piccadilly in the West End of London, and then later at the Royal Lodge in Windsor Great Park. She and her sister Margaret used to play hopscotch and hide-and-seek, but their main game was playing horses. For treats they used to go for walks in Hyde Park, and one of the staff in the household remarked that they would come back rather puzzled as to why so many strangers waved at them. He had to remind them that it was because they were Princesses. Much of the time the girls were under the watchful eye of their nanny, Allah (Mrs Clara Knight), Bobo MacDonald and her sister Ruby. People have attributed the Queen's thrifty nature to Bobo, who encouraged her to fold up and keep used Christmas paper as a child and to go around turning off unnecessary lights, especially later, during the war.

Princess Elizabeth was taught how to read by her mother at the age of five, and later on a governess, 'Crawfie' (Miss Marion Crawford), was brought in to teach the Princesses the basics of English, maths, music, drawing and other skills deemed appropriate. The girls also took French and dancing lessons.

Their grandmother, Queen Mary, was concerned that they also be well versed in the history of the monarchy and the Empire, and were fully aware of what was expected of them as members of the royal family. Queen Mary was stern and thought that smiling in public was not something that royalty should do too often. But their grandfather, King George V, was a surprisingly playful figure. He is said to have taken quite a shine to his first female grandchild, playing games with her and giving her the nickname Lilibet, which is still her family name.

Elizabeth was determined from an early age. In 1928, when she was two, Winston Churchill described her as being 'a character. She has an air of authority and reflectiveness astonishing in an infant.' She was described as 'charming and unselfish', whereas Margaret, her younger sister, was thought by adults to be 'naughty but amusing'.

'Crawfie', who later started the habit of writing the royal kiss-and-tell stories that plagued the family throughout the second half of the twentieth century, described Elizabeth's passion for order and procedure. 'The two little girls had their own way of dealing with their barley sugar. Margaret kept the whole lot in her small, hot hand and pushed it into her mouth. Lilibet, however, carefully sorted hers out on the table, large and small pieces together, and then ate them daintily and methodically.' This fetish for tidiness used to lead her to jump out of bed several times a night to check that her clothes and shoes were still neatly arranged. The historian Kenneth Rose noted, 'That early regard for order and routine has proved useful to the constitutional monarch.'

Princess Elizabeth and her younger sister Princess Margaret had a happy childhood in London, Windsor and Scotland.

In 1936 Elizabeth suddenly became heir to the throne because her Uncle David decided, after his accession as Edward VIII, that he could not bear to live without the woman he loved, the twice-divorced American, Wallis Simpson. Until the last moment, the British press censored word of the affair, news of which which was rife in the USA and Europe. This crisis, when it became public, divided the nation. There were those who sympathized with the King. The government, the Church of England and all the Commonwealth prime ministers were certain: he must choose between throne and love. He chose love, was given the title Duke of Windsor and went into exile.

On 10 December 1936 Edward VIII's abdication became law. Cheering crowds gathered outside 145 Piccadilly, the house of his younger brother Bertie, who suddenly, and to his dismay, was King. Like many others, he was frightened that he would not be up to the task. Inside the house, his eldest child, Elizabeth, learned why the crowds were there. She rushed to tell her sister, Margaret, who asked, 'Does that mean that you will have to be the next Queen?'

'Yes, some day,' Elizabeth replied.

'Poor you,' said Margaret. The next day, Crawfie claimed, Elizabeth and Margaret curtsied to their father for the first time. 'He stood for a moment, touched and taken aback. Then he stooped and kissed them both warmly.'

Their mother, who now became Queen, never forgave the Duke and Duchess of Windsor for thrusting her husband into this unexpected role, and for forcing the monarchy into a crisis that many thought would destroy it. No British sovereign had ever before voluntarily abdicated; the deed was an assault on every principle of hereditary monarchy.

In the event the royal switch was carried out with remarkably few problems. When finally presented with the crisis, the people of Britain were shocked, but they seemed more eager to have a monarch than anything else, and were delighted that the new one already had a Queen and two charming children. It seemed correct that the arrangements for the coronation planned for Edward VIII were not changed – 'Same date, new King'. To underline the sense of continuity, Prince Albert deliberately chose the name of his father and was crowned George VI. At the coronation, Winston Churchill (who had supported Edward VIII against the government) turned to his wife Clementine with tears in his eyes and said, 'You were right; I see now the "other one" wouldn't have done.'

The new King was determined to show that duty was the quality in which he set most store. And duty was what his eldest daughter imbibed from him. 'If you see someone with a funny hat, Margaret, you must *not* point at it and laugh,' Elizabeth told her more wayward sister. Duty was thrust upon her by the abdication and it has remained her mantra ever since. One of her teachers, Vicomtesse de Bellaigue, said later that 'Elizabeth had an instinct for the right thing. She was her simple self, *très naturelle.* And there was always a strong sense of duty mixed with *joie de vivre* in the pattern of her character.' (Vicomtesse de Bellaigue became the Princess's friend as she grew up, and remained a hugely important influence on her until her death in 1995.)

Princess Elizabeth wrote an account of her father's coronation on 12 May 1937 which she dedicated to her parents. 'At 5 o'clock in the morning I was woken up by the band of the Royal Marines striking up just outside my window. I leapt out of bed and so did Bobo... There were already some people in the stands and all the time people were coming to them in a stream with occasional pauses in between. Every now and then we were hopping in and out of bed looking at the bands and the soldiers...'

She was old enough to appreciate something of the majesty and the mysticism of her father's coronation, a ritual that stretches back in English life to the early days of the Anglo-Saxon kings. One close childhood friend said that Elizabeth did change after the coronation – although she was still able to have and be fun, she became more responsible.

The royal family moved to Buckingham Palace, where efforts were made to keep life much the same as before. Nothing was to happen to 'us four', the strong family unit of King, Queen and the two Princesses. They had a guide troop at the Palace, and girls of suitable ages and background were invited to join. They included Patricia Mountbatten, who was slightly older and remembers that Princess Elizabeth was her second in command: 'I was patrol leader and she was my patrol second, and she was an extremely efficient and capable patrol second, I well remember.'

It is in times of national crisis, particularly war, that the monarchy comes into its own. Of course a president or a prime minister can lead a country well in time of war, and many do. But a monarchy provides a neutral focal point above and beyond politics with which people can identify their fears and their beliefs more easily. Fighting and, if necessary, dying for King and Country seemed, certainly in those days, almost part of the natural order.

Mindful of this symbolism, the King and Queen vigorously rejected the idea that any of the family should go into exile during World War II. Harold Nicolson, the politician and diarist, met them over lunch in July 1940. The Queen said to him that 'personal patriotism is what keeps us going. I should die if I had to leave.' He was surprised when she told him that she was being instructed every morning on how to fire a revolver. 'Yes,' she said, 'I shall not go down like the others.'

'I cannot tell you how superb she was,' Nicolson wrote to his wife, Vita Sackville-West. 'I anticipated her charm. What astonished me is how the King is changed. He is now like his brother. He was so gay and she so calm. They did me all the good in the world. How I wish you had been there. *We shall win.* I know that. I have no doubts at all.'

Elizabeth and Margaret spent the war first in Scotland, which they loved, then at Windsor Castle. The Castle was blacked out and its paintings and treasures removed. Elizabeth was put through a more rigorous education than hitherto, with the Vice-Provost of Eton, Henry Marten, teaching her the basics of constitutional history. Marten was an exciting and enthusiastic teacher who inspired in her a great admiration for Queen Victoria.

Early in the war a German plane crashed in Windsor Great Park, and Buckingham Palace was bombed, leading to the Queen's celebrated comment: 'I'm glad we've been bombed. It makes me feel I can look the East End in the face.' (The East End of London suffered particularly heavy bombardments.) Princess Margaret later recalled wartime at Windsor Castle: 'After tea we would play games, something like that, and then we'd have supper because we were quite young and then we'd go to bed. Then the siren would go and we'd be woken up and dressed – probably in a siren suit and we'd set off on the long trot down the corridor, down the stairs, along another passage underneath, and then down the cold stone steps to this shelter which is at the bottom of the tower.'

It was during the war that Princess Elizabeth fell in love with Prince Philip of Greece, a young naval officer five years older than her. He was a great-great-grandson of Queen Victoria. His father, Prince Andrew of Greece, and his mother, Princess Alice of Battenberg, sister of Lord Louis Mountbatten, were exiled from Greece when he was 18 months old and thereafter he had no real home. His parents did not stay together and his childhood, at school in Britain,

The King and Queen, with the Prime Minister Winston Churchill, inspecting bomb damage at Buckingham Palace in 1940.

was unsettled, though he spent time with the English branch of his family.

One childhood friend, Georgina Wernher, now Lady Kennard, with whose family he often stayed at Luton Hoo, said, 'He was very rumbustious, full of fun ... But he did have a terribly sad background. He had no home to go to, nobody to kiss him good night... He never whinged, but it must have been awful not to have love. In those days, he had only the coat he stood up in, and certainly no suit because my parents bought him one...' Many of his friends have said that this childhood made him build a protective shield around himself. Bishop Michael Mann, the former Dean of Windsor, told the *Daily Telegraph*, 'His childhood experience taught him to be cautious, to swallow his feelings. And what he did was build a picket line around himself, with machine guns on it. You are not admitted through that line unless you are totally trusted.'

At Cheam Preparatory School he was good at sports. At the Scottish public school, Gordonstoun, founded by the educationalist Kurt Hahn, he became head boy and showed that he was both well liked and a natural leader. He developed a love for sailing, and first met Princess Elizabeth in 1939 at Dartmouth Naval College where he was a cadet. During the early part of the war, he served in the navy and she wrote to him frequently. In 1941, Philip earned a mention in dispatches after the Battle of Matapan in the southern Peloponnese. He came to see her in the Christmas pantomime, *Aladdin*, that was put on in Windsor Castle in 1943. 'I have never known Lilibet more animated,' wrote Crawfie. 'There was a sparkle about her none of us had seen before.'

By the time of Elizabeth's eighteenth birthday, in 1944, Philip was serving as second-in-command in the destroyer *Whelp*. He visited her at Balmoral that summer. The same year Queen Mary, Elizabeth's grandmother, told a friend that Elizabeth and Philip 'had been in love for the past 18 months' but the King and Queen felt that she was too young to be engaged. They felt that she should be meeting other eligible young men at parties, especially when the war was over. However, Elizabeth, unlike her mother and her sister, was not really a party person. Her biographer Sarah Bradford quotes a friend as saying, 'She was a shy girl who didn't find social life easy... She quite enjoyed it once she could get going but it didn't come absolutely naturally to her, she hadn't the temperament and needed confidence.' She gained that confidence towards the end of the war when she joined the Auxiliary Territorial Service (ATS) and learned how to dismantle and service heavy vehicles, a task she performed with obvious pleasure. This was her first opportunity to mix with and judge herself against other people.

VE Day was celebrated with wild abandon in London on 8 May 1945. The two Princesses stood with their father and mother on the balcony at the front of Buckingham Palace, and they waved and waved to the exultant crowds, who called them back onto the balcony eight times. Then Elizabeth and Margaret insisted that they be allowed to celebrate in the streets and not just in the Palace. Reluctantly and nervously the King agreed, and they slipped out of a side door of Buckingham Palace with a small group of friends and ran up and down St James's Street with thousands of others. One of the party was Lord

Princess Elizabeth learned the trade of mechanic as a member of the Auxiliary Territorial Service during the war.

The royal family and Winston Churchill stood on the balcony of Buckingham Palace to acknowledge rapturous crowds in The Mall on VE Day – 8 May 1945 – the day the war in Europe officially ended.

Porchester, later Lord Carnavon, who recalled, 'We went off and walked into Parliament Square and up Whitehall, down Piccadilly. There were people jostling and sailors with drinks in their hands, it was quite an astonishing atmosphere. And then I remember we went into the Ritz Hotel through one door and out the other… We were arm in arm like everyone else – seven or eight people walking down the street together.'

When they got back to Buckingham Palace, the Princess spotted one of her staff in the crowd and asked if he would go inside and tell the King and Queen that they were outside in the crowd. Lord Carnavon remembered that, 'In a few minutes they all began to shout "We want the King, we want the King". Finally the King and Queen came out on the balcony and the roar that went up was really a very exciting moment and I think Princess Elizabeth enjoyed the hustle and bustle of what was going on in the streets and will always remember it.' Indeed she later said, 'It was one of the most memorable nights of my life.'

The streets of London were filled with revellers on VE Day. Princesses Elizabeth and Margaret slipped out of the Palace incognito to celebrate amongst the crowds.

Philip continued courting Elizabeth after the war and she fell ever more deeply in love with him. Some in the Palace did not take an immediate shine to this confident young man, even though he now had a good war record. Edward Ford, then Assistant Private Secretary to the King, first met Philip in 1946 when everyone became aware that he was Princess Elizabeth's intended. 'He never showed the respect that an English boy of his age would have had for the older people around. He had no retiring graces... Everyone thought, "This rough diamond, will he treat the Princess with the sensitivity she deserves?" ' But Ford also noted that although Philip was poor, he was not greedy. Other courtiers and some young men who saw themselves as potential suitors to the Princess made their hostility plain to the interloper. One said, 'He is not an English gent.' But the King liked him and saw him for what he was – rather opinionated and brash: an independent man.

His friend and aide, Michael Parker, later told the writer Graham Turner that 'The thing he was most looking for when he came to Britain was a home... So when he told me that he'd become engaged to Elizabeth, he was extremely content, though not way over the top.' An unnamed close friend told Turner that the Princess was 'mad about him, though she never showed her feelings in public. She needed someone like him, someone who was his own man, and she realized it.'

In 1946, her parents allowed her to become privately engaged to Philip. But they thought that she was still too young and, to her dismay, insisted that the news should not be announced until after the family had completed a tour of South Africa in early 1947. The Princess was not pleased at being parted for so long from her fiancé. She was and remained deeply in love; Philip was to be a vital part of her life through all the decades to come.

While they were in South Africa, she marked her twenty-first birthday with a speech to the Commonwealth, in which she made what she called 'a solemn act of dedication' that came to seem fundamental to her entire life. In a filmed radio broadcast she stated: 'It is very simple. I declare before you that my whole life, whether it be long or short, shall be devoted to your service and the service

In South Africa in early 1947, the two Princesses rode the footplate of the royal train.

Princess Elizabeth became formally engaged to Prince Philip of Greece in July 1947.

of our great Imperial Commonwealth to which we all belong.' Just as important as these often-quoted remarks was the following request: 'But I shall not have the strength to carry out this resolution unless you join in it with me, as I now invite you to do; I know that your support will be unfailingly given. God bless you all who are willing to share it.' In 1947 the Princess could, with confidence, state that she knew that people's support would be given unfailingly but that became less axiomatic as the country changed over the coming decades.

On 8 July 1947, soon after the family's return to London, her betrothal to Philip was announced. It was, for the most part, welcomed as a love match, although some newspapers muttered about the times being very austere. They were – though standards of living were rising. Clement Attlee's Labour government, which had ousted Churchill at the end of the war, had embarked on a radical programme, but there were still serious postwar shortages and rationing of basic foods, quite apart from Britain's underlying structural problems.

Winston Churchill sent his congratulations and the Princess thanked him, writing, 'We are both extremely happy, and Philip and I are quite overwhelmed by the kindness of people who have written sending us their good wishes.' Churchill wrote to the King that the news had certainly given 'the keenest pleasure to all classes'. 'The marriage will be an occasion of national rejoicing, standing out all the more against the sombre background of our lives.'

They were married on 20 November and many people remarked that the celebration, muted though it was in deference to the times, was bright enough to briefly lift the postwar gloom. After the ceremony in Westminster Abbey, the couple set off (with one of the Princess's favourite corgis) by train to Broadlands, the home of the Mountbattens. But they were not left in privacy, and to escape photographers and gawpers they moved on from Hampshire to Scotland.

The Princess's father wrote to her of the pride he had felt in giving her away. He was thrilled to walk up the aisle with her, 'but when I handed your hand to the Archbishop I felt I had lost something very precious. You were so calm and composed during the Service and said your words with such conviction that I knew it was all right. I can see that you are sublimely happy with Philip which is right, but don't forget us is the wish of Your ever loving and devoted PAPA.'

For Philip (who was created Duke of Edinburgh just before the marriage) life became very different, and rather difficult. In the navy his life had been simple and independent rather than lavish and formal. He did not find the new constraints of Court life easy, but both he and his wife thought that he would be able for many years to develop his career, assume command of his own ship, and keep protocol at bay. Elizabeth believed that as a mere Princess she could be a wife and then a mother.

She quickly became pregnant and Prince Charles was born just a year after their wedding, on 14 November 1948. Crowds gathered outside Buckingham Palace to read the notice posted on the railings. A friend of mine remembers the headmaster of his boarding school bursting into the dormitory at midnight, shouting, 'Princess Elizabeth has been safely delivered of a baby son. God Save the King!' Queen Mary gave to her great-grandson a silver cup that had belonged to her great-grandfather George III.

The Princess's marriage in November 1947 caused great excitement in a country only just emerging from the shadow and sacrifice of war.

The year after Prince Charles's birth, Prince Philip was posted by the navy to Malta, where his wife joined him. For a few months they lived happily as naval officer and wife. Elizabeth's cousin Margaret Rhodes said, 'I personally think the happiest times for her must have been her very early married years, when she was just a naval officer's wife in Malta. It was her first sort of contact with leading an absolutely ordinary life, and I don't think she did very much in the way of royal duties.' She went shopping, to the hairdressers, and enjoyed the company of other naval wives. She and Philip were utterly relaxed. In August 1950 their second child, Anne, was born in London.

By now the Princess was helping her increasingly sick father more and more. She found the constant meeting and greeting of strangers a strain; it came more naturally to Philip. In October 1951 the young royal couple undertook a tour of Canada, and included a visit to the United States. At first the Princess looked tired and distracted, but soon the excitement built up. America was a huge success, with President Truman in Washington announcing that 'Never before have we had such a wonderful couple, that so completely captured the hearts of all of us.' Years later, Martin Charteris told the Queen's biographer Ben Pimlott that Truman 'fell in love with her'. This became something of a pattern.

In October 1951 the Labour government was defeated and Winston Churchill returned to office. The King admired the simple rectitude and determination of Clement Attlee, but each was so shy that communication between them was hesitant. Churchill's return was easy for the King – the old wartime partnership was happily re-established. Only a few months later, Churchill's grief on hearing of the death of the King was very real.

Prince Charles was born in November 1948, Princess Anne in August 1950.

After Edward Ford had broken the news that the King had died, Churchill's aide Jock Colville (who had worked for Princess Elizabeth) went into the Prime Minister's bedroom. 'He was sitting alone with tears in his eyes, looking straight in front of him and reading neither his official papers nor the newspapers. I had not realized how much the King meant to him. I tried to cheer him up by saying how well he would get on with the new Queen, but all he could say was that he did not know her and that she was only a child.'

The long, bumpy flight that brought the new Queen back from Africa was the mirror image of the journey out, with sadness and trepidation replacing joy. Captain Ballantine recalled that she had flown out as 'a beautiful, fun-loving young woman, and going back she had grown up completely and was now worried about the responsibility of being Queen'.

She changed into her mourning clothes on board the plane at the last moment, as if to defer reality as long as possible. She called Martin Charteris to sit with her and asked him, 'What happens when I get there?' As the plane taxied to a halt at London airport, she saw that the big black Palace cars had been sent to fetch her. 'Oh, they've sent the hearses,' she said, using the term that she and her sister had always used for the big royal limousines. One of her most sympathetic biographers, Elizabeth Longford, suggested that 'the words were a lament not only for her father's death but for the death of her own youth...at twenty-five her personal carefree life was over'. Pamela Mountbatten thought that this was the moment at which the Queen finally realized the enormity of what had happened, and how her life had changed.

A number of officials boarded the plane when it landed. One of them was carrying a box containing a small, black feathered hat. All in black, the new Queen walked alone down the steps of the plane, her hand resting lightly on the handrail. The image of the frail, beautiful young figure descending to her destiny is extraordinarily poignant. At the bottom of the steps stood the political leaders of her land: Churchill and Attlee, Foreign Secretary Anthony Eden, and others who had come to greet her, including her father's brother, the Duke of Gloucester.

The young Queen returned home immediately after the unexpected death of her father. At the bottom of the plane's steps stood Winston Churchill, Clement Attlee and other officials. She and Prince Philip were then driven to London.

The Queen and Prince Philip managed a few smiles – perhaps more than one would have expected – and then they climbed into one of the 'hearses'. A photographer caught an image of the Queen sitting in the corner, her head cast down, looking sad and contemplative. In his own car Churchill was dictating a radio broadcast on the King to be made that night. He was in floods of tears and remained so for much of the day. In his broadcast he was at his most eloquent, describing the man he saw as 'a devoted and tireless servant of his country'. The announcement of the King's death, Churchill said, 'struck a deep and solemn note in our lives which, as it resounded far and wide, stilled the clatter and traffic of twentieth-century life in many lands and made countless millions of human beings pause and look around them.'

There was great truth in this. I remember being in the garden at home with my mother weeping as she told me that the King had died. Like millions of Britons, she wore a black armband for a month after the King's death.

Churchill's sentiments, on this as on many occasions, epitomized the monarchist feelings that prevailed in a country where at least a third of the people thought the Queen had been chosen by God. 'The King,' Churchill said, had 'walked with death, as if death were a companion… In the end death came as a friend; and after a happy day of sunshine and sport, and after "good night" to those who loved him best, he fell asleep as every man or woman who strives to fear God and nothing else in the world may hope to do.'

Now the 'Second Queen Elizabeth' was ascending the throne, at the same age as the first, nearly 400 years earlier. The Prime Minister said he was looking forward to his new Queen. 'I, whose youth was passed in the august, unchallenged and tranquil glories of the Victorian era, may well feel a thrill in invoking, once more, the prayer and the anthem: "God Save the Queen".'

That evening, Elizabeth's grandmother, Queen Mary, came to pay her respects; the 84-year-old woman, who had lived through five reigns, curtsied to her young granddaughter. The next day, 8 February 1952, the public proclamation of the new sovereign was read by the Garter King of Arms at St James's Palace and the Queen had to appear before the Accession Council, where she read her Declaration of Sovereignty, impressing her elders with her calm demeanour. She and Prince Philip then drove to Sandringham to join her mother and Margaret, and to pay respects to the body of her father. A few days later her mother, announcing that she now wished to be called Queen Elizabeth the Queen Mother, said, 'I commend to you our dear daughter; give her your loyalty and devotion; in the great and lonely station to which she has been called she will need your protection and your love.'

Protection and love. She had both. In his speech to Parliament on the death of the King, Churchill said of the new Queen's reign 'we must all feel our contact with the future'. And he added, referring to the gathering clouds of the Cold

George VI's coffin was brought by train from Sandringham to King's Cross station in London. Tens of thousands of people attended his lying in state.

Three queens in mourning for the King – his daughter, Elizabeth, his mother, Mary, and his wife, Elizabeth.

War, 'She comes to the throne at a time when a tormented mankind stands uncertainly poised between world catastrophe and a golden age… If a true and lasting peace can be achieved and if the nations will only let each other alone, an immense and undreamed of prosperity with culture and leisure ever more widely spread can come, perhaps even easily and swiftly to the masses of the people in every land. Let us hope and pray that the accession to our ancient throne of Queen Elizabeth the Second may be the signal for such a brightening salvation of the human scene.' The Commons was electrified by such oratory.

The King's funeral took place on 16 February at St George's Chapel, Windsor. The card on the Government's wreath read 'For Valour' (as for the Victoria Cross). It was in Churchill's hand. The image that remains is of the three queens – Mary, Elizabeth the Queen Mother and Elizabeth II – all three faces covered with black veils, standing near the coffin, together in their loss but each alone in her reveries of the past, and hopes and fears for the future.

Later that year the new Queen talked about her forthcoming coronation day and said, 'I want to ask you all, whatever your religion may be, to pray for me on that day – to pray that Christ may give me wisdom and strength to carry out the solemn promises I shall be making, and that I may faithfully serve him, and you, all the days of my life.'

She had consecrated her life to her people. Churchill thanked her, saying, 'We are resolved to prove on the pages of history that this sacrifice shall not be made in vain.'

two

The New Elizabethans

It has been said that the past is another country. But Britain in 1952 is another world. We were still a nation recovering from the immense exertion of World War II; there were bombsites all over London and other great cities. Added to the expense of rebuilding were the costs of nationalization and the welfare state embarked upon by the radical Labour governments of 1945–51, and accepted by the Conservatives.

Politicians then were towering figures. Churchill and Attlee each had their enemies and critics but they had buried their party differences and united behind the war effort. People were far less cynical about their leaders than they are now.

The monarchy was not just accepted but adored by the overwhelming majority of the population. It was seen as the hub of national unity, the central link in a changing world, the natural focus of love and allegiance. Even those who did not consider it God given believed the Crown to be one of the vital features of British life and society.

Britain was a Christian land. The Church of England, a pillar of the monarchy and society for centuries, was literally a tower of strength. When the Queen came to the throne there appeared to be a revival of Christian belief. From 1945 to 1958 church membership, Sunday School enrolment, Easter Day communion, baptisms and religious marriages all dramatically increased. There was the greatest church growth that Britain had seen since the mid-nineteenth century. The American evangelist Billy Graham had remarkable success on his crusades of 1954–6.

There was, in those early postwar years, a vigorous reassertion of the 'traditional values', including thrift and sexual restraint, the role of women as wives

◁ The coronation portrait of the Queen in Westminster Abbey by Cecil Beaton captured the glory and the weight of history upon her.

and mothers, and moral panic over 'deviancy' and delinquency. According to Callum Brown, author of *The Death of Christian Britain*, 'The mental world which produced this in the 1950s was not just a world of a tiny minority…[it] was a national culture, widely broadcast through books, magazines and radio, and deeply ingrained in the rhetoric with which people conversed about each other and about themselves. It was a world profoundly conservative in morals and outlook, and fastidious in its adherence to respectability and moral standards.' Everyday lives were still deeply affected by Christian symbols, authority and activities. Children who did not believe in God were denounced as 'heathen' in playgrounds. John Lennon's mother 'lived in sin' and this made him the object of constant jibes at school.

The strength of religion meant that sexual morals were strict. Fifty-five per cent of men and 73 per cent of women disapproved of women having sex before marriage. Young lovers lived in terror of pregnancy. One writer has described the 'official culture' of the period as a kind of 'psychic dam' imposed by the establishment through the Lord Chamberlain's censorship of the theatre, the courts' censorship of literature and the Reithian concepts that guided the new medium of television as well as radio. Suburban ordinariness was enjoyed by older generations as the prize for having survived and won two world wars. Britain was dominated by values that today are seen as old fashioned. They can perhaps be summed up by the notions of 'duty' and 'service', which the Queen personified then as she still does today. The armed forces were hugely important. Two years of national service were a normal part of life for every teenage boy.

In 1952 the writing may have been on the wall for heavy industry, but it was obscured by centuries of grime and soot. The British economy was still dominated by steel, shipbuilding and mining. The service and media industries were in their infancy. The television era was just born. There was only one channel, the BBC, and few homes had television sets. It would be many years before the medium came of age and transformed society.

Britain was an overwhelmingly white nation. The first immigrants from the British colonies, particularly the West Indies, had begun to arrive in 1947, but there were still only 36,000 a decade later. Class divisions had been diminished but not ended by the war. Social rank was easily identified by accents and clothing, even by men's hats.

But alongside the apparent certainties there were great anxieties in the early 1950s. The new Conservative chancellor, R.A. Butler, admitted in 1952 that the country faced 'a major calamity for sterling'. This was to be the lament of government after government for the next 30 years. Meanwhile, Europe was more and more rigidly divided between east and west by the Iron Curtain. Behind it the Soviet Union and its communist satellites were creating states of terror that they seemed eager to replicate on our side, given the chance.

And then there was the Empire and Commonwealth. The British Empire, the greatest the modern world has seen, once covered 13 million square miles and embraced over 360 million people. When the Queen was crowned, she could make a world tour and scarcely leave her own territories. But the age of Empire was over. The question now was whether Britain could replace it with something that could meet the worldwide cries for independence and self-government – the Commonwealth.

The era of decolonization had begun with the end of World War II. In 1947 and 1948 India, Pakistan and Ceylon each became self-governing dominions. In 1950 India moved further away and became a republic but, crucially, its leaders elected to remain within the Commonwealth. Gone was any notion of the King as Emperor of India. From now on India would owe no allegiance to the King, but would acknowledge him as Head of the Commonwealth; he would now be the symbol of Commonwealth unity. The King, saddened by the loss of India from the Empire, spoke encouragingly of such changes: 'Our Commonwealth – the British Commonwealth – has been subject to the laws of evolution. We would not have it otherwise.' The Queen herself said, 'The Commonwealth bears no resemblance to the Empires of the past. It is an entirely new conception…'

In 1952 there were eight members of the Commonwealth, including Britain. Six were self-governing nations – Canada, Australia, New Zealand, South Africa, Pakistan and Ceylon – all of which retained the British monarch as their head of state (unlike India). At the first Commonwealth Prime Ministers' Conference of the Queen's reign in December 1952, the members agreed that the Queen would be crowned as 'Elizabeth the Second, by the Grace of God of the United Kingdom of Great Britain and Northern Ireland and of her other Realms and Territories Queen, Head of the Commonwealth, Defender of the Faith'.

At the beginning of her reign, the Commonwealth was not a concept that many people understood. It did not really become significant until the process of

There were just eight members at the first Commonwealth Prime Ministers' meeting in 1952. The Queen has nurtured the institution, which by 2002 had 54 members.

Since 1952, the Queen has always made her Christmas broadcast a personal message to the peoples of the Commonwealth.

decolonization, which accelerated in the 1950s, transformed what remained of the colonial empire into a grouping of independent sovereign states. These states retained a relationship with the Queen, who was sometimes their head of state but more commonly the Head of the Commonwealth. It is now one of the most successful international groupings in the world.

In the Queen's first Christmas broadcast in 1952 she stressed, 'We belong, all of us, to the British Commonwealth and Empire, that immense union of nations, with their homes in all four corners of the earth. Like our own families, it can be a great power for good – a force which I believe can be of immeasurable benefit to all humanity.' Her coronation six months later was an international affair that cemented Commonwealth bonds.

Kenneth Kaunda, later to be President of Zambia, remembers that at her coronation he organized 'quite a few boycotts' in Northern Rhodesia (as Zambia was then called) since the Queen represented the British rule that he was fighting against. Zambia became an independent member of the

Commonwealth in 1964. After 27 years of working with the Queen, he believes, 'The transformation of the British Empire to a Commonwealth was an achievement made possible without hesitation, I'd say, because of the personality of Queen Elizabeth. Without that, many of us would have left.'

Throughout her reign, the Commonwealth has been the Queen's greatest political passion; she speaks of it as a family. As we shall see, her fight to represent and to embody the Commonwealth has run parallel with her struggle to represent her own people. It is a fight that has been crowned with success — indeed, it is one of the enduring achievements of her reign.

Prince Philip, together with the Earl Marshal, the Duke of Norfolk, was put in charge of organizing the coronation. The Prince needed the task; it was harder for him than for anyone else to adjust to the realities of his and the Queen's new status. He was an independent and strong-willed man and had, until now, been the head of his family. Now he was incarcerated in Buckingham Palace, a place that no resident seems to feel is a home. He sometimes felt that he was just a spare wheel. He found many of the courtiers very stuffy as well as very old. He was also upset when told that he would not be allowed to change the family name from Windsor to Mountbatten. Queen Mary was determined that the name should remain unchanged, and Churchill, who felt no great affection for Lord Mountbatten, the principal supporter of the change, called a meeting of the Cabinet, which authorized him to advise the Queen that Windsor was the preferred name.

The Queen, meanwhile, was becoming more relaxed. Elizabeth Longford records that she confided to a friend after her accession, 'Extraordinary thing, I no longer feel anxious or worried. I don't know what it is – but I have lost all my timidity, somehow becoming the Sovereign and having to receive the prime minister, for instance.' She was lucky in having in her first prime minister an old man with vast experience, wit and eloquence, who quickly came to love her.

The date of the coronation needed to be chosen. Churchill was against it being held in 1952 because the country's economic crisis was so serious that he felt that not a single working day should be lost. 'Can't have coronations with the bailiffs in the house,' he said. So early summer 1953 was mooted and eventually Tuesday 2 June, the day before Derby Day, one of the highlights of the horse-racing calendar, was chosen.

The young Queen was initially wary of having the ceremony televised; she hated the idea of cameras continually being trained on her. It is not surprising, then, that Jock Colville, Churchill's Private Secretary, wrote a memo that concluded: 'The Committee [the coronation Joint Executive] was almost unanimous in considering that television of the actual ceremony should not be allowed… Whereas film of the ceremony can be cut appropriately, live television would not only add considerably to the strain on the Queen (who does not herself want TV) but would mean that any mistakes, unintentional incidents or undignified behaviour by spectators would be seen by millions of people.' The Prime Minister, the Archbishop of Canterbury and the Westminster Abbey clergy all backed the Queen.

However, when the news broke that the coronation would not be televised there was widespread dismay. In October the decision was reversed, with the proviso that the Queen should not be shown in close-up. According to Colville's later account, it was the Queen's initiative, and she told the Prime Minister that 'all her subjects should have an opportunity of seeing it'. Churchill and the Cabinet acceded. 'After all,' he said, 'it was the Queen who was to be crowned, not the Cabinet.' The decision had a huge impact on the nascent television industry. People scrambled to buy television sets in preparation for the big day, and others were converted to the new medium by the event itself. Churchill was determined that everyone should enjoy themselves. He insisted that rationing of sweets and chocolate must end before the coronation. He was warned that there would be a severe shortage of sugar, but he refused to accept this advice. Rationing was dropped, and in the event there was a glut of sugar.

As the coronation approached, so did an extraordinary sense of anticipation in the country. Houses were painted red, white and blue. People prepared street parties. Some called it hysteria but it was not that, rather a sense of excitement and vindication – the immense effort and sacrifice of the war were now to be rewarded in the crowning of a beautiful young Queen, a unique symbol of what people hoped was to be a national rebirth or regeneration. There was much talk of a New Elizabethan Age. The historian A.L. Rowse declared robustly that the idea was 'silly…a mere matter of nomenclature'. But to many the idea of the New Elizabethans was irresistible.

Over one million people came into London to see the procession or the decorations, and to imbibe the celebratory spirit. The mood of congratulation heightened when news came through the day before the coronation that Mount Everest had finally been conquered by a Commonwealth team. 'All This – And Everest Too' rejoiced the *Daily Express*.

The coronation was the twenty-eighth to take place at Westminster. The ceremony goes back to the earliest days of the Anglo-Saxon kings. In the eighth century it already contained the same essential elements it retained in the twentieth century – the anointing of the monarch, the hand-over of the emblems of power (including the Sword of State, the Orb, and the Sceptres of Power and Mercy) and enthronement. The Queen was to be crowned with St Edward's Crown, made for Charles II, but the crown that she wore for the return to the Palace was the one made for Queen Victoria.

Coronation day dawned dank and drizzly. But that had not deterred thousands of people from sleeping on the streets, along which the Queen was to pass in the Gold Coach to and from her coronation. The roar of the crowd was continuous and exhilarating.

The dignitaries in Westminster Abbey had been there since early in the day. One remembers, 'There was a sort of hush and I think we all felt that something exciting was about to happen. And then suddenly three little ladies in blue overalls appeared from I don't know where, with enormous hoovers which they again plugged in…and proceeded to hoover the blue carpet that led from the door right up to the throne…there was something most gloriously incongruous about it.' But finally they heard 'in the distance crowds cheering and getting nearer and nearer and nearer'. Then the Queen was at the doors of the Abbey. She was accompanied by six maids-of-honour. One of them, Lady Anne Coke, now Lady Glenconner, remembers that 'The Queen was amazingly calm. Once

The vows that the Queen made at her coronation have governed her life ever since: 'The things which I have here before promised, I will perform and keep. So help me God.'

we got the train and everything was arranged, she just looked behind her and said "All right, girls" and off we went.'

The essence of the ceremony is Christian but it also contains elements of older, almost primeval, rituals of sacrifice and dedication. The service began with the Archbishop of Canterbury declaring to the bishops, 'Sirs, I here present unto you Queen Elizabeth, your undoubted Queen', which was followed by cries of 'GOD SAVE QUEEN ELIZABETH' and the sounding of trumpets. The 'solemn promises' that she was asked to make were far reaching and, for her, life-long. The Archbishop swore her to 'Govern the Peoples of the United Kingdom of Great Britain and Northern Ireland, Canada, Australia, New Zealand, the Union of South Africa, Pakistan, and Ceylon, and of your Possessions and the other Territories to any of them belonging or pertaining, according to their respective laws and customs'. She swore also to judge with Law, Justice and Mercy, to maintain the Laws of God, and to 'preserve inviolably the settlement of the Church of England'. Laying her hand upon the Bible, she said, 'The things which I have here before promised, I will perform and keep. So help me God.'

While the choir sang the anthem 'Zadok the priest and Nathan the prophet anointed Solomon king…', which Handel composed for the coronation of King George III, the most moving and sacred moment of the service took place. Her crimson robe was removed and, in a simple white shift, she was anointed with holy oil by the Archbishop. He declared that she was now 'anointed, blessed, and consecrated Queen over the Peoples, whom the Lord thy God hath given thee to rule and govern…'

The anointing, according to the Archbishop, brought her 'into the presence of the living God'. For her this moment was the most solemn of her life. Jane Vane Tempest Stuart (now Lady Jane Rayne), one of the maids-of-honour, said of the anointment, 'I think that moment is etched on my memory for ever…she looked so vulnerable, rather like a novice nun in a very simple shift.' Anne Coke was so moved at that moment that she remembers saying a prayer for the Queen, that 'her reign would be a long and happy one'. Such prayers were said by millions across the land.

There was one brief moment of light relief during this very serious ceremony. The peers of the realm came to pay homage to the Queen, and one lady of the bedchamber noted, 'Prince Philip was first, and he must have made some amusing little joke, because it was the only time she smiled in the whole ceremony.' Her promises were heard not only by the 7,500 peers, churchmen, politicians and foreign and other dignitaries in Westminster Abbey but also by the huge crowds that lined the streets and the 27 million people who watched the coronation live on television in Britain alone. Betty Brown, then a 22-year-old confectionery saleswoman from the north of England, said, 'If you had a television, everyone came to see it, so on coronation day my aunts and uncles and cousins all gathered in my mum's house – and we watched it enthralled. My mum made a buffet – roast ham, pease pudding, beef, custard pies and cake – and we watched the ceremony and nobody spoke.' The ceremony was an act of national communion.

On the balcony of Buckingham Palace after the coronation it seemed that the vast crowds below expressed 'a surge of love' for the Queen.

When the royal party returned to the Palace they had their photographs taken. One maid-of-honour recollects, 'The Queen sat down and lifted off her crown, which weighed a ton, I believe. She put it on the table and Prince Charles came tearing along and picked it up and put it on his head, and promptly fell over, crown and all.' When the party went out onto the balcony the whole of The Mall, right up to Admiralty Arch, was crammed with people. One in the party remembers looking down on the 'seething mass of humanity' and having 'this feeling of such warmth and admiration coming from them, welling up' as they expressed this 'surge of love' towards the Queen.

This feeling of rebirth and unity also stretched abroad. Film of the coronation was seen by hundreds of millions of people around the world within days. Christian Dior said, 'The coronation of the young Elizabeth II had filled not only the British but, rather strangely, the French too with renewed faith and optimism in the future.' According to *Time* magazine, 'The whole world is royalist now', and the Queen held that world in her hands.

On the evening of the coronation, the Queen broadcast to the nation. She was introduced by Churchill, who said, 'The words "gracious" and "noble" are words familiar to us all in courtly phrasing. Tonight they have a new ring in them because we know they are true about the gleaming figure whom Providence has brought to us, and brought to us in times where the present is hard and the future veiled.'

Following the coronation, the Queen was determined to be seen by as many of her subjects as possible. She embarked on a series of tours at home and

On the 1953–4 Commonwealth tour, her longest voyage ever, the Queen and Prince Philip travelled to Australia in SS *Gothic*.

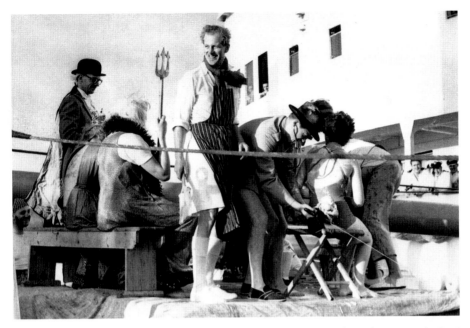

Prince Philip joined in the high jinks on board SS *Gothic* during the traditional 'Crossing the Line' ceremony in December 1953.

abroad. In November 1953 she and her husband and a number of close aides, including Pamela Mountbatten and Mike Parker, set off on a five-and-a-half-month tour of the remaining Empire and the growing Commonwealth. They visited Bermuda, Jamaica, Fiji, Tonga, New Zealand, Australia, the Cocos Islands, Ceylon, Uganda, Malta and Gibraltar. This was the journey that had originally been devised for King George VI, and was begun by the Princess and Prince Philip in January 1952 – the journey that ended in Treetops. Now, instead, it was undertaken by a young Queen whose beauty, dutifulness and vulnerability had touched the world. Her purpose, she said, was 'to see as much as possible of the people and countries of the Commonwealth and Empire, to learn first hand something of their triumphs and difficulties and something of their hopes and fears'. Furthermore, 'I want to show that the crown is not merely an abstract symbol of our unity but a personal bond between you and me.'

The first stops were Bermuda and Jamaica, where they boarded SS *Gothic* for a three-week cruise through the Panama Canal and across the Pacific Ocean to Fiji and Tonga. They crossed the equator, calling for much fun as the ritual of the 'Crossing the Line' had to be observed. Those who had never crossed the equator before were put in seats, lathered and shaved by the ship's barber and then tipped into the ship's pool. Prince Philip participated eagerly in this ceremony and the Queen filmed it from a safe distance. She herself had already crossed the line on her trip to South Africa in 1947; on that occasion she and Princess Margaret were only required to have their noses dusted with a powder-puff.

In Fiji, native chiefs gave the Queen a whale's tooth. She was impressed by their traditional welcome, which consisted of sitting on the ground, clapping hands and grunting three times. Pamela Mountbatten remembers the Queen practising this on the floor of *Gothic* – 'At that moment, of course, one of the stewards came in and was transfixed in the doorway seeing the Queen sitting grunting and clapping on the floor.'

In Tonga, the Queen was welcomed by the other queen of the Commonwealth, Queen Salote. She had become a firm favourite of the British crowds during the coronation when she insisted on keeping her carriage uncovered in the pouring rain on the way back from the Abbey so that the crowds could see her. While in Tonga the Queen and Prince Philip were driven around in the London taxi that Queen Salote had brought home after the coronation, and they stayed in the Queen's Palace that she had vacated for their visit. It reminded some of an old Victorian boarding house. Pamela Mountbatten noted in her diary

The original wirephoto caption from November 1953 reads: 'Jamaica beams on the Queen...at a youth rally called to greet the royal couple.'

And in December, 'The great moment for Fiji when the royal visitors land on Fijian soil.'

that the Queen and Philip were not overjoyed to be woken at dawn one morning by a symphony of nose flute music from the garden. She described a feast for about 700 people: 'We ate with our fingers and there were no implements of any kind. The food was unbelievably delicious and excellently cooked. There was roast suckling pig, still warm from cooking, and very tender crayfish, yams, chicken and turkey, breadfruit, watermelons, pineapples, some rather less appetizing Tongan sweet wrapped in soggy leaves, and coconut drink.' The Queen was not known for her appetite, but she 'gallantly did the best her small appetite would allow and was able to spin it out for some while'. She knew 'that as the person of highest rank, when she stopped eating everyone else would also have to stop'. Queen Salote had tears running down her face as she said goodbye.

Gothic docked in Auckland on a drizzly day, but this did not diminish the enthusiasm of the crowds. Graham Stewart was a young photographer sent by his paper to capture the moment the Queen stepped ashore. He described her arrival as 'like the second coming'.

The New Zealanders arranged for 200 children to come to Government House and present Christmas presents for Prince Charles and Princess Anne who were at home in London. The Queen gave her second Christmas broadcast live from New Zealand – a triumph of engineering for the BBC wireless men involved.

She talked about the notion of 'a New Elizabethan age' saying, 'Frankly, I do not myself feel at all like my great Tudor forebear, who was blessed with neither husband nor child, who ruled as a despot, and was never able to leave her native shores'. But she did remark that, 'There is at least one very significant resemblance between her age and mine. For her kingdom, small though it may have been and poor by comparison with her European neighbours was yet great in spirit...'

From Auckland the royal party set off on a long tour of the North and South Islands, stopping in remote villages and towns. They were greeted everywhere with joy. The Maori, for whom the Queen felt a particular regard, performed their dances of welcome. Huge crowds waved and carried placards. One read, 'God bless the Queen and keep an eye on the Duke'. Pamela Mountbatten noted

Queen Salote of Tonga had won the affection of the British public during the coronation. She was a generous hostess to the Queen and Prince Philip.

at the time, 'The National Anthem is always sung, and there is something very moving about people's emotion at having their first opportunity to sing "God Save the Queen" with the Queen standing in front of them.'

In Palmerston she met the Dunedin Ladies' Brass Band, the only female brass band in the Commonwealth. Nancy Byrne, the drum major, remembers the excitement. 'Growing up during the war, we had no sort of idols…we didn't have a girls' pop group or a singer. So we looked up to the little princesses, and if they wore a frilly dress, well, our mothers gave us a frilly dress. If they wore twin-sets, Mum would knit me a twinset, or a pleated skirt, whatever it was… And when the Queen was married, it was wonderful. We went to the movies to see these sorts of things because there was no television. And then this lady appeared in front of me. I just couldn't believe that she was there and I was seeing her. And it was just a wonderful, wonderful feeling.'

Nancy Byrne met the Queen again 37 years later at a garden party held in Christchurch, New Zealand. She and her aunt were introduced to the Queen. She recalls, 'My aunt, overwhelmed by the occasion, said, "Oh, but Nancy met you when you came to Palmerston last time." And the Queen looked at me and said, "Ladies' brass band." "Yes, Ma'am," I replied.'

For some people, though, seeing the Queen once or twice just wasn't enough. She was taken aback when one woman popped her head through the car window and announced, 'That's the twenty-fifth time I've seen you.'

Jock Phillips, then six, saw the Queen 10 times: 'I can remember being dressed up in my posh gear, still carrying a Union Jack, and…standing there with four or five other cousins on the back of this truck. And we raced along beside the royal train.' They got off at each stop to see the Queen, then got back on the truck and raced her to the next destination. One sheep farmer dyed his sheep flock in red, white and blue, and stood them out beside the train track.

The Queen was very moved when *Gothic* finally pulled away from New Zealand on 30 January 1954 and thousands of people turned up to say farewell. Next stop, Australia. Sydney Harbour 'was alive with boats', recalled Pamela Mountbatten. 'Ferries festooned with people were so top-heavy on the side nearest *Gothic* that their decks were level with the water and it seemed preposterous that they did not sink.' The city was no less impressive; the decorations were said to have cost £2 million. Ivy Reid camped out all night to get a good spot. She remembers, 'We had to mind our place because we were sitting in the gutter…but everything that went up and down Macquarie Street that night got a wave and a cheer from all the people who were there, and there were hundreds there in the night. In the morning, there were thousands.' When the Queen arrived 'we could hear the cheering in the distance, and it was gradually getting louder and louder… And then you'd hear them coming up Castlereagh Street, oh, it was the most exciting thing you've ever seen.'

It was a punishing schedule. The Queen and Prince Philip travelled the length and breadth of Australia, meeting dignitaries, making speeches, unveiling plaques, eating dinners, making polite conversation and conducting investitures. An astonishing three-quarters of the population came to cheer her. She wanted the motorcades to travel slowly so that people could get a proper view. 'What's the point of coming, unless they can see me?' she asked.

Noel Haupt was a police officer awarded the British Empire Medal for rescuing a family who had nearly drowned when their car fell into a river. The Queen delighted Haupt by knowing about what he had done. He was touched

Everywhere in New Zealand and Australia, huge crowds turned out to see the Queen and Prince Philip. One man said, 'It was like the second coming.'

that 'She'd taken the trouble to acquaint herself with the particular aspects of the rescue'.

The tour was slightly disrupted by scattered outbreaks of polio. In some towns where the disease was a risk, the Queen and the Duke remained on the observation platform while speeches were read out. Hands were not shaken, which must have been a welcome respite.

The royal party did get to spend a day on the Great Barrier Reef, but the most interesting sights were deemed to be too dangerous. Pamela Mountbatten recalls that the Queen, 'eaten alive by creepy crawlies and insects', was not in the best of spirits. She was, however, considerably cheered when a boatload of trippers appeared on the scene gesticulating wildly and shouting whether anyone had seen the Queen. 'The Queen,' said Pamela Mountbatten, 'leapt to her feet and dashed down to the edge of the beach and pointed to the far end of the island, yelling, "She went thataway, she went thataway." And then she jumped up and down on the beach with joy when the boat disappeared round the corner.'

At times she felt the strain. Smiling constantly is both exhausting and difficult – it gave her a tic. She knew that when she did not smile she looked cross, even though she was not. She also had to be adept at avoiding the thorns of roses and wooden sticks on small flags thrown into the royal cars by well-wishers. And the same small talk hour after hour, day after day, place after place was wearing. However, the impact that the Queen had on the people of Australia was huge. As Pamela Mountbatten reflected, 'You could hear the emotion in the voices of the old soldiers who would come up to one and, still gazing at the Queen, say quite simply, "Now we know what we fought for."'

They left Australia in April 1954. The voyage home included Ceylon, where the Queen opened Parliament in her coronation gown. This time, however, the glass beads on her dress heated up so much that she later said it was 'like being in a radiator'. The trip continued via the British Protectorate of Aden on the Red Sea and the East African colony of Uganda. Under an umbrella protecting her from the sun she said to Prince Philip, 'I feel like an African Queen.'

'You *are* an African Queen,' he replied.

From Uganda they flew to Tobruk, Libya. There they joined the new royal yacht *Britannia,* which had sailed from England with the young Prince Charles and Princess Anne aboard. The Queen always felt rueful about leaving them for so long – this was the first great sacrifice of her reign. In those days it would have been thought extraordinary if she had brought her children along; today it would be considered natural. Later she joked, 'They were extremely polite. I don't think they knew who we were at all!' Film taken by the Queen and Prince Philip shows them all on deck having a great time on an improvised slide, with Charles conducting the band of the Royal Marines.

As *Britannia* steamed towards Malta, the British Mediterranean fleet under the command of Lord Mountbatten provided the escort. From Malta it was home via another outpost of the Empire, Gibraltar, and then north to England. Winston Churchill clambered aboard off the Isle of Wight. That evening, he fell

Winston Churchill was the Queen's first and favourite prime minister. Their meetings were 'always such fun', she said.

asleep as they watched a film. The Queen woke him and bade him goodnight saying, 'I hope you sleep well.' He replied, 'Now we have you home, Ma'am, I shall sleep very well.'

The Prime Minister stood with his sovereign on the bridge as the ship steamed up the Thames towards London. There was a tumultuous welcome, with crowds lining the banks of the river, and cranes in the position of salute. Churchill was, as ever, eloquent. 'One saw this dirty commercial river as one came up,' said the Queen later, 'and he was describing it as the silver thread which runs through the history of Britain.' He saw things 'in a very romantic and glittering way; perhaps one was looking at it in a rather too mundane way'.

In his official address of welcome to the Queen on her safe return, Churchill said, 'Even Envy wore a friendly smile... I assign no limits to the reinforcement which this royal journey may have brought to the health, the wisdom, the sanity and the hopefulness of mankind.'

The Queen replied that the monarchy could easily be archaic or meaningless, but on her tour, 'We have received visible and audible proof that it is living in the hearts of the people.' That was 1954. Her challenge would be to keep it alive through all the years of her reign.

three

Constitutional
Monarch

The Queen came to the throne poignantly young, but she understood the job rather well, having learned at her father's knee. She knew that the monarch has many duties, some formal, others more intangible. He or she is head of state and head of the nation.

The point of a constitutional monarchy is that it places the position of head of state beyond political competition. Above and beyond the political fray, the monarch is supposed to represent the whole nation to itself. That is its core function.

Power resides in theory in Parliament, in practice with the government of the day. But the monarch remains the ultimate constitutional arbiter. The monarch's remaining constitutional powers are first to appoint the Prime Minister and second to agree or refuse a dissolution of Parliament. The politician who commands the majority in the House of Commons must go to the Queen to be invited to form a government and become Prime Minister. The Prime Minister also has to ask the monarch's permission to call an election. In times of political crisis, if there were a hung Parliament or if the government were to act unconstitutionally, the monarch has to act. He or she is the ultimate check on government. The nineteenth-century writer and authority on government Walter Bagehot noted: 'The Sovereign has, under a constitutional monarchy such as ours, three rights — the right to be consulted, the right to encourage, the right to warn.'

Just how the Queen has exercised those rights on a constant basis is unknown. Perhaps her diary will eventually inform us, when it is read after her death. One of the golden rules is that state papers and diaries are kept completely locked away until the next reign. Even her own diary may not reveal much;

◁ The State Opening of Parliament by the Queen is one of the most important fixtures in the constitutional calendar.

she is said to take the view that her confidential discussions should not be recorded for posterity.

Her great-grandfather Edward VII, grandfather George V, uncle Edward VIII and father George VI had each faced serious constitutional problems, including Ireland, women's suffrage and abdication, to name but three. The testimonies of her forebears show that there has been ample scope, within the constitutional limits, for the monarch to put his or her views to the Prime Minister. Members of the royal family have often had strong opinions. Victoria held prejudices that she never hesitated to express to her ministers. If she were to have a real row, she would sometimes say, 'I'll abdicate. I'll go to Australia.' Her dislike of William Gladstone, whom she tried to keep out of office, fortunately never became public; Gladstone himself behaved impeccably in concealing it.

In 1884 Queen Victoria was far more interested in the condition of the poor than most of her politicians, and she pushed for the creation of a royal commission on 'The Housing of the Working Classes' on which her son, the Prince of Wales, sat. Her intervention was also crucial in settling the struggle over the extension of the right to vote. Sir William Harcourt commented that it showed 'how powerful is the influence of the Crown, constitutionally exercised, to avert by its authority and mediation, dangerous political conflicts'.

The principle that monarchs act only on the advice of ministers was now well established. They must do that, Asquith noted to Victoria's grandson George V in 1910, 'whether that advice does or does not conform to the private and personal judgement of the Sovereign. Ministers will always pay the utmost deference, and give the most serious consideration, to any criticism or objection that the Monarch may offer to their policy, but the ultimate decision rests with them; for they, and not the Crown, are responsible to Parliament...'

George V's most important contribution to political life was his benign and public acceptance of the first Labour government in 1924 – because, he said, 'they should be given a fair trial'. In 1931 he did play an important part in persuading Ramsay MacDonald to form the National Government to defend the pound. It was in many ways a disaster, but the King's belief that the people wanted at least a notional national coalition to confront the economic crisis was borne out by

The Queen's official boxes, filled with documents to be read or signed, are with her every day of every year.

the triumph of the National Government in the 1931 election. Nothing demonstrated the power of the prime minister over the monarch more clearly than the abdication crisis, when Stanley Baldwin told Edward VIII in 1936 that he could not marry Mrs Simpson and still be King.

George VI was perturbed by the coming of socialism in 1945. In the words of the historian Peter Hennessy, he 'peppered' Clement Attlee with his 'reservations about the intrusiveness of the state in the lives of his subjects'. He had a temper and used to get into what his family called 'a gnash' if he felt he was not being adequately informed on government policies. Some of Attlee's briefing papers for his Tuesday talks with the King have been declassified. They show that the subjects the Prime Minister most often raised were the Empire and Commonwealth, followed by other foreign affairs and European co-operation (even then), the economy and trade, and domestic affairs. The Soviet Union rated only two mentions.

Michael Adeane, the Queen's longest-serving private
secretary, was a voice of caution.

There are no formal, written rules governing the relationship between
monarch and prime minister. When the Queen acceded in 1952, she had to feel
her way. At first, she relied for guidance on her Private Secretaries. Of these, the
longest serving was Michael Adeane, who worked with her from 1953 to 1972.
Adeane was an important influence on the Queen. He had a reputation for being
cautious and rather stuffy. He carried a notebook on constitutional practice, and
made it his job to keep the Queen out of politics as much as possible. Martin
Charteris, his assistant and then successor, once told me, 'If I had had the job
earlier, I would have found politics hard to resist. Michael got her going on the
side of constitutional rectitude, which suited her well. I would have been
inclined to let her have her head more. He was right, but it made life more boring.'

The relationship between the Queen and her Prime Minister is at the heart of
the constitution. Central to it is the regular weekly meeting between the two;
every Tuesday evening when both monarch and premier are in London they
meet to discuss the determining factor in any Prime Minister's life – 'events'.

The Queen has had 10 prime ministers in five decades – as many as Queen
Victoria had in 63 years. Over the half-century of her reign, change has been
phenomenal, almost revolutionary. In all that time, one might say, the only
constant has been the Queen. It is impossible to quantify the influence that
the Queen has had on her premiers. They have all been remarkably discreet,

while praising her experience, knowledge and understanding. None has broken the rule that what is said at their weekly conversations remains completely private. But it is clear that the meetings impose a discipline. Each week, the Prime Minister has to marshal his thoughts in order to explain his policies. As the historian A.J.P. Taylor wrote, this is important: 'To make the Prime Minister explain himself is a useful task, often beyond the wit of Parliament to accomplish.'

The Queen did once say what she thought she was able to do for her Prime Ministers at these meetings. 'They unburden themselves or they tell me what's

The Queen in 1985 with Prime Minister Margaret Thatcher and five of her predecessors: James Callaghan, Alec Douglas-Home, Harold Macmillan, Harold Wilson and Edward Heath.

going on, or if they've got any problems, sometimes one can help in that way too. They know that one can be impartial... I think it's rather nice to feel that one's a sort of sponge and everybody can come and tell one things. And some things stay there and some things go out of the other ear and some things never come out at all. One just knows it... And occasionally [one is] able to put one's point of view [and] perhaps they hadn't seen it from that angle.'

Her earliest mentor was, of course, Churchill, and in some ways he remained her favourite prime minister. Each was overawed by the other – he by her loveliness and youthful eagerness to learn, she by his long and victorious life. There is something touching in the image of the old warrior tutoring the young Queen in the art of governance. Later she said that her meetings with him were 'always such fun'. They were often long. Once, when he was asked what they talked about, he replied, 'Oh – racing.'

Soon after the coronation Churchill had a major stroke, which his doctors and senior Conservative Party leaders concealed. At first he was not expected to live, but he not only survived, he continued in office for another two years. There were those, both in the Conservative Party and at Court, who thought that the Queen might have used one of their regular Tuesday evenings to urge him gently towards the exit. She did not; in fact she continued to 'encourage' him.

She asked Churchill and his wife Clementine to the St Leger at Doncaster races for their forty-fifth wedding anniversary soon after his stroke. They were then invited to Balmoral, a sojourn that their daughter Mary described as 'a target and a test'. He passed it and returned home much heartened by his own powers.

By this time, though, there was more glory than realism in Churchill. He was less interested in the pressing economic and structural problems of the country, and more concerned to retain some vestiges of its imperial greatness. Britain's main problem then, and for decades thereafter, can be summed up in one phrase – chronic economic crisis. Churchill, the fierce and realistic critic of appeasement abroad, did not really confront the economic enemies at home. When finally he decided to step down, the Queen sent word that, 'she felt the greatest personal regrets, and that she would especially miss the weekly audiences which she has found so instructive and, if one can say so of State matters, so entertaining'.

Winston Churchill adored his young Queen; she dined with him at 10 Downing
Street just before he resigned in April 1955.

On 4 April 1955 Churchill gave a farewell dinner at Downing Street for the
Queen. His words were, as ever, exquisite. 'I have the honour of proposing a toast
which I used to enjoy drinking during the years when I was a cavalry subaltern
in the reign of Your Majesty's great-great-grandmother, Queen Victoria.' He
thanked her and Prince Philip for the inspiration that they gave throughout the
realm and Commonwealth. 'Never have the august duties which fall upon
the British monarchy been discharged with more devotion than in the brilliant
opening of Your Majesty's reign. We thank God for the gifts He has bestowed
upon us, and vow ourselves anew to the sacred causes and wise and kindly
way of life of which Your Majesty is the young, gleaming champion.'

Consider that phrase, a 'wise and kindly way of life'. It was a delightful way of
describing Britain in 1955, but it was a description that might seem increasingly
archaic as the reign progressed.

The next day Churchill was driven to the Palace to submit his resignation. The Queen asked if he would recommend a successor; he said he preferred to leave it to her. There was a choice – Harold Macmillan, R.A. (Rab) Butler, and Anthony Eden, the Foreign Secretary, all had plausible claims for advancement. The Conservative whips favoured Eden. The Queen called for him and asked him to try to form a government. She told Churchill that if he ever wanted to leave the Commons she would like to offer him a dukedom.

She wrote to him in her own hand, 'I need not tell you how deeply I felt your resignation last Tuesday, nor how severely I miss and shall continue to miss, your advice and encouragement.' While she had complete confidence in Eden, 'It would be useless to pretend that either he or any of those successors who may one day follow him in office will ever, for me, be able to hold the place of my first Prime Minister, to whom both my husband and I owe so much and for whose wise guidance during the early years of my reign I shall always be so profoundly grateful.'

When Churchill died in January 1965, she accorded him the honour of a state funeral. She provided his wife, Clementine, and family with carriages and hot-water bottles for the journey to St Paul's Cathedral. She also broke with protocol and attended the service – not only that, but she insisted that the Churchill family rather than she should have the honour of arriving last at the Cathedral. Years later, in 1973, when Churchill's statue was unveiled in Parliament Square, the Queen asked that Clementine Churchill should pull the cord. 'For more than 50 eventful years,' she said, 'Lady Churchill was his deeply loved companion and I think it would be right, therefore, for her to unveil the statue of her husband.'

Anthony Eden won the election in May 1955, but his administration was troubled. He was not well enough for the job and any lingering romance of the New Elizabethan Age had vanished. Dock strikes and rail strikes led Eden to ask the Queen to declare a state of emergency. The 30-year nightmare of wretched industrial performance was upon the country. From now on, trade, balance of payments, interest rates, sterling crises, union power and rates of production were the stuff of which government and everyday life were made. And then there was the drama of Eden's intervention at Suez.

In July 1956, Gamel Abdel Nasser, the dictator of Egypt, nationalized the Suez Canal Company. Eden, who had resigned as Foreign Secretary in 1938 in protest at the appeasement of Mussolini, believed that it would be wrong to appease Nasser. The French and the Israelis were equally alarmed, and the three powers secretly colluded on an invasion of Egypt designed to remove Nasser.

It is not known whether Eden told the Queen in advance, at one of their Tuesday meetings, about the conspiracy. She might well have been dismayed, knowing that it would anger the other nations of the Commonwealth. Years later, when a newspaper published an article claiming that she was opposed, Eden was furious. He told Robert Lacey, the author of *Majesty*, that she did not disapprove of the operation, but he also said 'nor would I claim that she was

Britain's last imperial foray was the invasion of Egypt in 1956. Its failure, in the face of American opposition, showed the retreat of British power.

Anthony Eden's Suez adventure ruined his health as well as his premiership.

pro-Suez'. She behaved entirely correctly in supporting her government; if she had qualms, she never showed them.

The Queen was in a difficult position. She had to support British troops in action – indeed she would have wanted to do nothing else. But nearly every member of the Commonwealth criticized the British policy. Washington, in the midst of the election between Eisenhower and Stevenson, was furious and began a run on the pound in order to force Britain to withdraw. The Queen's closest advisers were divided on the merits of this imperial adventure in the post-imperial age. Her Private Secretary, Michael Adeane, was in favour of the operation, but the Assistant Private Secretaries, Martin Charteris and Edward Ford, were against it. Such is the discretion of Palace life that they did not, says Ford, make their views clear to the Queen.

Eden's health suffered further during the Suez storm. He flew to Jamaica to recuperate and Rab Butler had to take over temporarily. He did well, withdrew British troops from Suez and attempted to repair relations with Washington. Butler came to know the Queen at this time and later told Robert Lacey that he was struck by her love of political gossip. 'She enjoyed evaluating to what degree the government had suffered a setback or had scored in points in political terms. She appeared totally to appreciate the personal ambition inspiring the political animal, and was fascinated by the length one would go to secure his own advantage at the expense of another.'

Eden went to the Palace to resign in January 1957. The Queen wrote to assure him that his record as a statesman 'which has indeed been written in tempestuous times, is highly valued and will never be forgotten'.

His reply showed the value that prime ministers place on their links with the monarch. He wanted to 'try to express what my Sovereign's understanding and encouragement has meant at a time of exceptional ordeal. It is the bare truth to say that I looked forward to my weekly audience, knowing that I should receive from Your Majesty a wise and impartial reaction to events which was quite simply the voice of our land.' He thanked her for her 'unfailing sympathy and understanding'.

The Queen now had another chance to use her prerogative in selecting the Prime Minister. In effect the choice was between Rab Butler and Harold

Macmillan. Most people expected Butler to get the job, particularly after his competent stewardship in Eden's absence. But the Tory elder statesman Lord Salisbury and the Lord Chancellor, Lord Kilmuir, interviewed each member of the Cabinet to ask whom they preferred. 'Wab or Hawald?' asked Salisbury. Most said Harold. The Queen asked Churchill's advice, and when Butler later asked him what he had said, Churchill replied, 'Well, old cock, you're not such a bad old thing. You looked after me when I was ill. But I told her to choose the older man. Harold's 10 years older than you.'

The Queen sent for Macmillan. He was acceptable to Parliament, and in that sense she had done her duty properly; it was not her job to second-guess the procedures of any party. But she was criticized for not having taken wider soundings and for allowing herself to be manipulated by Salisbury. Some people continued to feel that a clique of Tory aristocrats had done Butler out of the job he deserved, and that the Queen had perhaps accepted this manoeuvre a little too easily and quickly. The Labour Party denounced the process. There were stirrings in the kingdom.

The Suez debacle opened all British institutions to reassessment. The year 1957 marked the beginning of the end of the magical monarchy the Queen had enjoyed since her coronation, and the beginning of what became a more sceptical relationship between Crown and people, Queen and country. There was love still, but it was not always unconditional.

In 1957 a young peer, Lord Altrincham (John Grigg) criticized the Queen in the small-circulation magazine the *National and English Review,* which he owned and edited. He described the Queen's speeches as being 'prim little sermons' and her style of speaking as 'a pain in the neck'. She sounded like 'a priggish schoolgirl, captain of the hockey team, a prefect, and a recent candidate for Confirmation'. Her background and training were too limited, and her advisers were not broadly enough chosen.

Because he was a Conservative and a peer, Altrincham's views created a furore. It was a slow August and the newspapers had a field day. The *Sunday People* published interviews with various members of the House of Lords, who said that their colleague should be administered various forms of brutal punishment: horsewhipping was one suggestion. He was in fact slapped in the street by an Empire Loyalist named Burbidge, who was charged for the assault. But the magistrate treated Burbidge leniently, fining him only 20 shillings and saying that most of the country was disgusted by Altrincham's article. The article was unprecedented because Altrincham had broken the taboo on direct criticism of the Queen. But his remarks were thoughtful and intended to be supportive of what he called 'the genius of constitutional monarchy'. He argued that it could not survive 'unless its leading figures exert themselves to the full and with all the imagination they and their advisers can command'. A poll in the *Daily Mail* showed that Altrincham's specific suggestions had more support than might have been expected.

He was right in saying that the monarchy 'cannot now rely, as it once could, upon the unquestioning support of those who effectively govern the country'. To survive, the monarchy would have to be above both race and class. He thought the Queen and her advisers were still too redolent of the upper classes, the debutante division. She needed 'a truly classless and Commonwealth Court'. Even some of the Queen's closest aides privately considered that such comments were helpful, and that it was time for the Palace to shed its 'tweedy' image.

As the 1950s gave way to the 1960s, a new kind of orthodoxy emerged, at least amongst the metropolitan elite. Deference began to die and was replaced by indifference, scepticism and satire. The satirical magazine *Private Eye* began life in 1961; one early cover pictured the Albert Memorial with the slogan 'BRITAIN'S FIRST MAN IN SPACE'. The play *Beyond the Fringe* and such BBC Television shows as *That Was The Week That Was* poked fun at the establishment. Inevitably, the monarchy came in for its share of criticism and mockery, though not yet abuse.

The Queen was clearly not unaware of the new youth movement that was forming. She said in 1961, 'It is natural that the younger generations should lose patience with their elders, for their seeming failure to bring some order and security to the world, but things will not get any better if young people merely express themselves by indifference or by revulsion against what they regard as an out-of-date order of things.' And, she added, 'the world desperately needs their vigour, their determination, and their service to their fellow-men'.

The first satirical sketch about the royal family was broadcast on *That Was The Week That Was* in March 1963. The programme's producer, Ned Sherrin, claims that it had in fact been commissioned by Princess Margaret, whom he met at a party: 'I think she'd been watching the programme. Anyway she said, "Why don't you do something about the ridiculous way that they report us?"' David Frost, the presenter, thought that a sketch called 'The Queen's Departure', performed by the Cambridge Footlights, fitted the bill. Sherrin remembers that the sketch 'simply describes the Queen in the Pool of London setting out in a barge which starts sinking. And as it sinks, the Dimbleby-esque commentary becomes more and more reverential until it finally finishes up, "The Queen is swimming for her life" and the band strikes up "God Save the Queen".' Although the sketch in no way ridiculed the royal family personally, it did mark a turning point for future satirists and comedians.

Chic and trendy London was one thing, but the Queen and her young family – Charles and Anne were followed by Andrew and Edward in 1960 and 1964 – were still very popular amongst the rest of the country. In retrospect, the 1960s were halcyon days for the Queen, days of innocence in which she took the most pleasure in her young family, her animals (as ever) and in building the Commonwealth on the foundations of the Empire.

One lady-in-waiting recalls that in the 1960s there were always crowds outside Buckingham Palace hoping to see the Queen. And large crowds still turned out wherever she went, all around the country.

Harold Macmillan was the first Prime Minister with whom the Queen was to have a long working relationship. He saw himself as rather grand, and shared the Queen's love of Scotland and field sports. He was witty, if pessimistic. She was able to lighten his often gloomy view of the decline of civilization. He found his weekly audience with her uplifting – indeed, it was one of the most enjoyable aspects of being Prime Minister. Macmillan was surprised by her.

'She is astonishingly well informed on every detail,' he wrote. He found that her views were as measured as his, but somewhat lighter – she could often cajole him out of his more morose moods. After one diplomatic failure, she wrote to console him and he replied, 'I hope I may say how heartened I was on my return to 10 Downing Street to receive the message…and I shall not conceal from Your Majesty the shock and disappointment which I have sustained.' He also found her determined to hold on to her constitutional privileges. When he wanted to appoint Butler as deputy prime minister, she refused, pointing out there was no such official post. Macmillan wrote in his diary that she had warned, 'I must not be accused of trying to appoint my successor, and thus injure the (royal) prerogative.'

In his memoirs, Macmillan emphasized the Queen's grasp of business and her thoughtfulness. He said of her, 'She does not enjoy "society". She likes her horses. But she loves her duty and means to be Queen and not a puppet.' He seemed to hanker for a more intimate relationship, as existed between Lord Melbourne and Queen Victoria, but she never gave that to any Prime Minister.

Macmillan was enthralled by the magic of monarchy. 'Imagine,' he once said, 'if at this moment, instead of the Queen, we had a gentleman in evening clothes, ill-made, probably from Moss Bros., with a white tie, going about everywhere, who had been elected by some deal made between the extreme Right and the extreme Left…! Then we would all wait for the next one, another little man, who is it going to be? … "Give it to X, you know he's been such a bad Chancellor of the Exchequer, instead of getting rid of him, let's make him the next President…" Can you imagine it? I mean, it doesn't make sense, that would be the final destruction of colour and life and sense of the past in this country, wouldn't it?'

Macmillan managed to put Suez behind Britain. He expanded the universities. Housewives began to acquire new labour-saving devices. The slogan 'Life's better under the Conservatives. Don't let Labour ruin it' helped him win the 1959 election, but it denied the underlying difficulties of the economy. Like Churchill, Macmillan was complacent about the way union power drove up inflation and eroded competitiveness. His period of office was strained by the country's continuing problems. Underlying the postwar consensus on economic manage-ment was the belief (or at least the hope) that the government could fund

Harold Macmillan, Chancellor of Oxford University as well as Prime
Minister, accompanied the Queen when she visited Oxford in 1960.

the welfare state while maintaining full employment. The writer Ferdinand
Mount, then a young Conservative Party helper, recalls a tour through Britain in
the early 1960s. 'It seemed as if nothing much had happened since the first industrial revolution. We passed miles of great sooty brick factories. Often with broken
windows stuffed with rags, apparently derelict, yet you could sometimes hear
the hum of ancient machinery and a dim light might be visible through the
murky panes… This odyssey was undertaken nearly twenty years after the end
of the war, but the sense of renewal was sadly absent.'

It was under Macmillan's premiership that Britain did most to transform
the Empire into a Commonwealth, a task in which the Queen was deeply
involved. In 1957, the first African colony won independence, when the Gold
Coast became the Republic of Ghana under the presidency of Kwame Nkrumah.
A remarkable pattern was becoming established: countries desperate to shake off
the shackles of the Empire proved equally eager to join the Commonwealth

India, once described as 'the jewel in the crown' of the British Empire, became a republic in 1950, but remained within the Commonwealth. The Queen was given a splendid welcome there in 1961.

once independence had been won. The Queen was integral to this process. She gave decolonization an air of dignity, and helped to establish a constitutional pattern. However difficult or divisive the battle for independence, two things were certain: a member of the royal family would be nominated by the Queen to attend the independence celebrations, and nearly all the new states would be welcomed into the Commonwealth.

Although British withdrawal was usually well managed, the survival of political regimes in these newly independent countries was often difficult. Many new countries fell apart. Some became dictatorships. Independence rarely brought good governance, especially in Africa.

In a speech in South Africa in 1960 Macmillan stated, 'The wind of change is blowing through this continent…and whether we like it or not, this growth in national consciousness is a political fact.' A clash between apartheid South Africa, governed only by whites, and the growing number of independent black African states was inevitable. The Commonwealth prime ministers met in London in May 1960. The atmosphere was highly charged, coming just weeks after the Sharpeville massacre in which South African police had killed 56 demonstrators. The participants said that the Queen helped diminish the anger felt on all sides at the meeting. But the South Africans were unwilling to abandon apartheid, and soon afterwards they voted in a referendum to become a republic and the country left the Commonwealth.

There is no doubt that the Queen was distressed by the rift – after all, it was in South Africa in 1947 that she had made her commitment to serve the Commonwealth all her life. But there was no alternative. Had South Africa

Despite safety concerns, the Queen visited Ghana in 1961 to the delight of its President, Kwame Nkrumah.

Two young and glamorous heads of state – the Queen and President John F. Kennedy – dined together with their spouses at Buckingham Palace in summer 1961.

stayed, the Commonwealth would have broken apart. Moreover, the Commonwealth was becoming a factor in the Cold War. The latest scramble for Africa between Moscow and Washington was increasingly intense in the early 1960s. The Queen became an important diplomatic weapon of the 'free world'.

In 1960 the Queen was due to visit Ghana but had to cancel because she became pregnant. Martin Charteris later told the historian Ben Pimlott that she said to him, 'I am going to have a baby, which I have been trying to do for some time, and that means I won't be able to go to Ghana as arranged. I want you to go and explain the situation to [President] Nkrumah and tell him to keep his mouth shut.' Charteris went to the Ghanaian capital, Accra, and was taken in to see the President. He went through the message twice, and was met with silence. Finally Nkrumah said, 'I put all my happiness into this tour... Had you told me my mother had just died, you could not have given me a greater shock.' Charteris said the Queen would try to visit in 1961.

In 1961 she toured Cyprus, India, Pakistan, Nepal and Iran, all countries on the rim of, or in some way targets of, the Soviet Union. The tour was a great success, and in India, to her delight, she was cheered by millions. As the historian Kenneth Harris pointed out, the tour showed that she could successfully be head of a Commonwealth that included monarchies, such as Australia and New Zealand, as well as the new republics.

By late 1961 there was growing opposition within Ghana to Nkrumah's dictatorship, and there was a real risk that he might, under Soviet influence, take the country out of the Commonwealth. Macmillan hoped that the Queen's visit would go ahead and that he could persuade President John F. Kennedy to invest in the West's multi-million dollar Volta Dam project to keep Nkrumah onside. He was nonetheless worried about the Queen's safety. She seemed less concerned. She told him she thought the world would be shocked if she did not go to Ghana and Khrushchev did. According to his Press Secretary, Harold Evans, 'Macmillan said, "What a splendid girl she is." She had been indignant at...the idea of having the trip cancelled. The House of Commons, she thought, should not show a lack of moral fibre in this way. She took very seriously her Commonwealth responsibilities, said the PM, and rightly so, for the responsibilities of the UK monarchy had so shrunk that if you left it at that, you might as well have had a film star.'

After bombs exploded in Accra, Macmillan sent the Commonwealth Secretary, Duncan Sandys (husband of Churchill's daughter Diana), there to determine whether the Queen would be safe. He said yes, and in the event the trip was a great success. One local paper called the Queen 'the greatest Socialist monarch in the world'. The British press applauded her courage. Macmillan wrote in his diary that, like Elizabeth I, 'she has indeed the heart and stomach of a man'. He immediately telephoned Kennedy and said, 'I have risked my Queen; you must risk your money.' Kennedy replied that he would match the Queen's 'brave contribution' with his own. The United States invested in the Volta Dam project and Ghana stayed within the Commonwealth.

In her Christmas broadcast that year the Queen spoke of her Commonwealth travels, and said how impressed she had been at the goodwill that existed between different peoples. She asked that problems be solved peacefully rather than in anger. She said, '"Oh hush the noise, ye men of strife, and hear the angels sing." The words of this old carol mean even more today than when they were first written.'

In the summer of 1963, the Macmillan government was dragged through scandal when the Minister for War, John Profumo, admitted that he had lied to the House of Commons when he denied his affair with a call-girl, Christine Keeler. Macmillan's handling of the crisis showed that he was, at the very least, out of touch. He wrote to the Queen 'to apologize for the undoubted injury done by one of Your Majesty's Secretaries of State... I had of course no idea of the strange underworld in which other people, alas, beside Mr Profumo have allowed themselves to become entrapped.' The Queen replied that she understood how hard it was for people of high standards to suspect colleagues of behaving improperly.

In October 1963, Macmillan, already deeply disheartened by the Profumo debacle, suffered a painful attack of prostatic obstruction. He thought this was the harbinger of cancer, and decided to retire. His sudden decision involved the Queen in one of the most controversial actions of her reign.

Macmillan presided over a Cabinet meeting just before his colleagues went up to Blackpool for the annual party conference, but he did not tell them how ill he felt. He then went straight into hospital. From there, on 9 October, he wrote to the Queen of his intention to resign. He called several of his colleagues to his bedside, amongst them the Foreign Secretary, Lord Home. He asked Home whether he intended to stand in his place; Home said he would rather stay at the Foreign Office. Macmillan had written a personal letter, announcing his resignation, which he asked Home to read to the conference in his capacity as its president. His successor was to be chosen by the 'customary processes'.

The Queen retained her prerogative to appoint the new prime minister, at least insofar as the Conservative Party was concerned. (The Labour Party had decided, after Macmillan was privately chosen to succeed Eden, that it would elect its own leaders in future.) Macmillan favoured either Lord Home or the Lord President, Lord Hailsham, to succeed. Each would have to renounce his peerage, but that had become possible because of the efforts of the former Lord Stansgate, now Tony Benn, the Labour MP. On the death of his father, Benn had forced a change in the law to allow him to renounce his inherited peerage so that he could remain in the Commons. Macmillan did not think that his deputy Rab Butler, who was now running the government as he had done during Eden's illness in 1957, was the man for the job.

Macmillan had his operation on Thursday 10 October. It was not cancer and he had good reason to regret his hasty resignation. By now a fierce race was developing for the succession. There was no shortage of plausible candidates. Lord Hailsham had immediately announced his intention to renounce his peerage and seek election to the House of Commons as Quintin Hogg. He had considerable support amongst the party at large, but his natural exuberance got the better of him and some felt, perhaps unfairly, that he disqualified himself when he spoon-fed his baby daughter on television.

Rab Butler was the choice of many who admired his years of distinguished service, his deliberate calm, and the fact that he was not an aristocrat. His problem was that he was not entirely trusted within his own party. He had dealt well with the aftermath of Suez, but the episode had split the Tories as well as the country and this harmed him. As the journalist and Cabinet minister William Deedes said later, Butler had an unfortunate way of disparaging his colleagues. Deedes thought Butler made himself look a much less trustworthy character than he really was. 'In a sense, nobody undermined him: he always undermined himself.' He never had the support of the majority of MPs, let alone party managers. The Chancellor of the Exchequer, Reginald Maudling, was more popular amongst MPs. And, despite his reservations, Lord Home now also allowed his name to go forward.

At the Tory conference, Maudling and Butler gave lacklustre performances. Home's speech, on the other hand, was 'a triumph' in the words of Philip Goodhart, then secretary of the backbenchers' 1922 Committee. Towards the end of the conference the executive committee of the 1922 Committee met. The Chief Whips of both the Commons and the Lords were there. Two members of the committee backed Maudling, two Hailsham and the other 10 members backed Home. None backed Butler. His supporters, who included the prominent MPs Enoch Powell and Iain Macleod, held a late-night meeting in London to demand that the Cabinet be re-consulted. Home, who had thought he was the unity candidate, called Macmillan to tell him that if he was dividing the party, he would withdraw. 'Nonsense,' said Macmillan.

That was the confused state of play as Macmillan sent his formal letter of resignation to the Palace on the morning of Friday 18 October. The Queen decided to visit her convalescing ex-Prime Minister in hospital. His physician, Sir John Richardson, wrote: 'The poor man had to have a bottle in bed with him, a bell by his side and Sister was outside the door in case he needed help while the Queen was there. He took all this, as everything else, with supreme detachment and dignity. He was very pale and tense and, indeed, unhappy...'

The Queen arrived in a blue-green coat and hat and, according to Richardson, spoke very softly. 'There were in fact tears in her eyes, and perhaps why I could not hear was because her voice was not very steady.' Macmillan was moved by her visit and wrote, 'She came in alone with a firm step and those

Alec Douglas-Home, Prime Minister from 1963 to 1964, shared the
Queen's love of Scotland and of country pursuits.

brightly shining eyes which are her chief beauty. She seemed moved; so was I.
I asked her leave to read her a memorandum which I had written yesterday and
brought up to date this morning. I said I was not strong enough to trust myself
to speak without a text.' Home, Macmillan told the Queen, was the party's
'preponderant first choice'.

Macmillan could be wry. Long afterwards, he reflected that it was 'an
extraordinary resignation…the bed covers were down, and concealed underneath the bed was a pail with a tube full of bile coming out of me… I made my
resignation to the Queen of England for an hour, in great discomfort.'

The Queen returned to the Palace and sent for Lord Home. He did not accept
the premiership at once, but said that he would 'try' to form an administration.
He knew he faced opposition in the party. The crucial question was whether
Butler would serve under him. Had he refused to do so, Butler's friends and
supporters would also have refused, and Home would have been unable to form
an administration. But at this vital moment in his career, Butler agreed to
become Home's Foreign Secretary. This reflected well on him; he might not have

won the ultimate prize but he still wished to serve. 'Bear in mind, the great thing is to be there…being part of public service,' Butler once said to William Deedes.

Butler's high-minded response – far less likely today than then – enabled Home to become Prime Minister. He renounced his peerage and became Sir Alec Douglas-Home. In the event, only Enoch Powell and Iain Macleod refused to serve under him. Hailsham and Maudling argued that since Butler was prepared to serve, they would too. However, the Queen was criticized for taking Macmillan's advice. Since he had resigned, many felt his views were no longer those of her Prime Minister and should not have been accorded any more weight than those of any other MP. She was also criticized for going to the hospital. Certainly it was unprecedented for the monarch to meet the premier in his pyjamas, but then it was unusual for a serving prime minister to resign while in hospital. The Queen was clearly doing her duty by saying she did not have to stand on ceremony. She took the view that Her Majesty's Government must be continued, and if Macmillan clearly could not come to her, she would have to go to him.

The Palace was not concerned about her visiting the Prime Minister's bedside; it was concerned that she should not make up the Conservative Party's mind for it. 'You choose, we send for' was the stated procedure. It is not the business of a constitutional monarch to become involved in the internal disputes of a political party. If the Queen had rejected Macmillan's advice and imposed her own choice, that is just what would have happened. By accepting Macmillan's advice and inviting Lord Home to see if he could form an administration, the Queen was telling the politicians that they had to resolve the business themselves. She scrupulously maintained the monarch's neutrality. It would have been a disaster if she had been seen to get involved in Conservative Party politics. Her constitutional duty was to appoint a prime minister who could command a majority of the Commons. As her Private Secretary Michael Adeane pointed out to the historian Kenneth Rose, it was not her duty to decide who was the best of several well-qualified candidates.

The Labour Party leader, Harold Wilson, denounced Home's appointment as the product of an aristocratic cabal. And the Tory MP Iain Macleod later wrote an article in the *Spectator* condemning the 'Magic Circle' of Tory aristocrats who had insisted that the post go to the old Etonian Earl of Home rather than the more humble Mr Butler. As a result of the crisis, Douglas-Home introduced new party procedures so that the Conservatives could in future elect their leader, thus removing from the Queen any further opportunity to use the monarch's prerogative.

The Queen praised Macmillan in her farewell letter. He had been her 'guide and supporter through the mazes of international affairs…you have had to unravel a succession of major and intricate problems affecting the peace of the world and the very existence of Britain and the Commonwealth. History will bear witness to the masterly skill with which you have handled them…' He replied, 'It is difficult to conceive of a more gracious and generous tribute from a sovereign to a subject.'

Alec Douglas-Home was close to the Queen. 'She loved Alec,' Martin Charteris told me. 'He was an old friend. They talked about dogs and shooting. They were both Scottish landowners, the same sort of people, like old school friends.' But there were those who thought it inappropriate that in the so-called 'swinging sixties' the Conservative Party should be led by the third old Etonian in a row, and they felt that this contributed to the Conservative defeat just a year later. But Home was manifestly decent, and in October 1964 he lost the election by only four seats (and very few votes) to the Labour Party, led by Harold Wilson.

The Queen was in a new era. For the first time she had a socialist Prime Minister, whose party, at least in theory, was less likely to accept the notion of monarchy than the Conservatives. Furthermore, the new government was pledged to embark on a programme of social reform, which, over the next six years, would help change attitudes and customs in Britain, perhaps more than at any other time in the century.

four

Changing People

It has been remarked that if George Washington and George III came back, Washington would be able to understand the job charged to President Bush, but George III would be nonplussed by the work of Queen Elizabeth II. One of any constitutional monarch's most important tasks is retaining consent. This involves the monarchy constantly adapting to change in the country, but the difficulty for the Queen has been that the changes in her reign have been so swift. She has always had to decide how fast to change because she cannot be seen to pander to nor be a follower of fashion. Yet consent must continually be earned.

The task is eased, somewhat, by the fact that monarchy is part of Britain's DNA. All countries need and have symbols. Americans have the flag. The French have 'la gloire' and the revolution. The British have the monarchy. And the royal presence is certainly felt in everyday life. It is even in the soap title *Coronation Street* and the thousands of real Coronation Streets up and down the country. Add to that the thousands more Jubilee Roads, Prince of Wales Drives and Victoria Places, and all the public houses named after Kings, Queens, Princes and Princesses. In the London telephone directory alone there are four pages and 12 columns of institutions called Royal, from the Royal Academy of Arts to Royal Worcester China. Every British postage stamp bears the Queen's head. All British money is certified by her image. Countless services and businesses with a royal warrant carry her crest.

The nation is affected by the Queen in a pervasive and constant way. All over the country every year, the police, civil servants, politicians, court officials, bishops, vicars and congregants swear the Oath of Allegiance to the Queen.

◁ During her Silver Jubilee year, 1977, the Queen was both surprised and moved by the clear affection expressed for her all around the country.

The monarchy is a focal point for their work. It is vital that the head of the nation is accepted, seen, heard, supported and embraced. And the nation is not just defined by geographical boundaries, but by the culture within those boundaries. This culture has changed considerably during the Queen's reign.

The Queen is aware of the difficulty of providing leadership. Early in her reign she said, 'In the old days the monarch led his soldiers on the battlefield and his leadership at all times was close and personal. Today things are very different. I cannot lead you into battle. I do not give you laws or administer justice. But I can do something else. I can give you my heart, and my devotion to these old islands and to all the peoples of our brotherhood of nations.'

At the beginning of her reign people felt deep affection for the Queen. This was expressed in the vast numbers who turned out to see her and in the letters that they sent her. On her father's death, they wanted to commiserate not just out of loyalty but empathy. Pamela Mountbatten, who helped sort those letters, particularly remembers those from women – young wives with young children – who said that they identified with the new Queen.

The contact that such letters provide is still important. The Queen receives about 200 to 300 a day, and many more when there is a royal wedding, birth or controversy. She looks at her post every morning, takes those letters she knows to be personal and makes a random selection of the rest. Some come back to her staff with notes and comments in the margin. 'I make a point of reading as many of them as I possibly can,' she said in 1987. 'I value all these letters for keeping me in touch with your views and opinions…'

Some letters ask for information about the royal family or are simply fan mail; others are more serious. Some are a pleasure to read, some are sad and some, she once said, 'are full of frank advice for me and my family', which 'do not hesitate to be critical'. Every letter gets a reply, either from a lady-in-waiting or private secretary, depending on the nature of the enquiry.

The Queen's position as Supreme Governor of the Church of England helps her give moral and spiritual leadership. Investing bishops, attending church festivals, memorials and thanksgivings does more than just put her in contact with Church of England congregants. It demonstrates that the nation has a spiritual agenda and priorities higher than the merely material or political. But as the Church has weakened, that signal has become more faint.

The head of a nation must also be seen to set standards in terms of personal conduct. In the latter part of her reign, her children have shown fallibilities, as we shall see, but the Queen's own conduct has remained above question. Furthermore, she sees it as her role to encourage ordinary people to do good works. In her 1954 Christmas broadcast she pointed out that although we rightly praise 'the heroes', sometimes behind them 'stand ranks of unknown, unnamed men and women willing and able, if the call came, to render valiant service'. She believes that the 'happiness and prosperity of the community' in great measure depends on her subjects who withstand 'constant small adversity'.

This is a theme that the Queen has repeated, mentioning 'the quiet people' who fight prejudice, stick to standards and 'make real sacrifices in order to help their neighbours'. She stresses her belief in the impact *everyone* can have – 'If enough grains of sand are dropped into one side of a pair of scales they will, in the end, tip it against a lump of lead. We may feel powerless alone, but the joint efforts of individuals can defeat the evils of our time.'

Twice a year, before the Queen's official birthday in mid-June and on New Year's Day, an honours list is published. On each occasion some 1,100 people are given honours to recognize their contribution to society – Knights of the British Empire, Commanders, Members and Officers of the Order of the British Empire and so on. All are intended to signify the sovereign's regard for different achievements.

The Queen does not choose many of the recipients. Most are nominated through a huge web of organizations and are scrutinized by the Civil Service. For the most part, honours are non-political, but every government has exploited the system for its own purposes, dispensing patronage to its supporters or those it wishes to attract. The Queen also has personal honours she can award, free of political interference, and these include the Orders of the Garter and the Thistle, the Royal Victorian Order and the Order of Merit. Most of the honours, political or personal, are awarded by the Queen herself or, increasingly, by the Prince of Wales at formal investitures.

As the critic Malcolm Muggeridge wrote, 'If the honours were conferred by a president or a prime minister, the odds are that they would lose some of their allure. The worthy alderman kneels ecstatically with creaking joints before the Queen to receive the accolade; the aged party hack finds one more canter in him when it is a question of being elevated...by Her Majesty in person.' The system is easily and often mocked, but those special trips to Buckingham Palace or Holyroodhouse in Edinburgh are enormously important to nearly all the recipients. Anthony Jay, the author of *Elizabeth R,* has noted that the system creates 'a feeling of national community focused on the Sovereign'.

The Queen also acknowledges people's achievements by sending letters of congratulations, presents and messages. Every centenarian receives a message of congratulation, as do couples celebrating their diamond wedding anniversary.

Recognition is also given through invitations to garden parties. These were started by Queen Victoria. Three are now held every summer at Buckingham

Every year the Queen invites about 40,000 people to garden parties at Buckingham Palace and Holyroodhouse, Edinburgh. Many guests are invited in appreciation of their work in the community.

The Queen's visits to hospitals, schools and charities are very important to those who work for them. Sustaining welfare institutions is one of the key aspects of the Queen's work.

Palace and one at Holyroodhouse. The Queen invites about 10,000 people to each party and meets about 200 during her progress through the garden. Sir William Heseltine, Press Secretary and later Private Secretary, says that in the 1960s 'there was a determined effort to broaden the categories of people who were invited', allowing 'a wider spectrum to be included'. Sir John Johnston who, as Comptroller of the Lord Chamberlain's office, helped arrange the garden parties in the 1980s, recalls that it was no longer 'just the Good and the Great or those who do a lot for charity, but a lot of the hard workers, like lollipop ladies'. Other changes were made to take into account new social norms: divorcees were invited and unmarried people could bring their partners and children.

In 1997, some 4,000 couples who had reached their golden wedding anniversary, as had the Queen and Prince Philip, were invited to a Palace garden party to celebrate. They reminisced about how many ration coupons they had needed for their wedding dresses. 'We were all in the same boat back in the 1940s,' several said to the Queen. She enjoyed the party greatly.

Since 1966 she has given the Queen's Award to Industry to 100 companies each year for significant achievements. She also recognizes the importance of thousands of people through her visits to hospitals, schools, factories and shows around the country. During each visit she is said to shake hands with some 30 to 40 people and meet many more in groups. By her presence she lends importance to the work of hundreds more doctors, teachers, factory workers, artists, and community and voluntary workers. It nearly always gives great pleasure; she has an effect that few politicians are able to match, much to their dismay. As Martin Charteris used to say, 'Darling, we are in the happiness business.'

The armed forces are another pillar on which the monarchy has traditionally been based. The Queen and her family are colonels in chief of many different regiments; it is a duty that they take seriously and which gives them much pleasure. Soldiers, sailors and airmen know that politicians send them into battle, but it is to the Queen that they swear an Oath of Allegiance. Whenever Britain is involved in combat, servicemen and women tend to write to the Queen, saying that they know they are fighting for 'Queen and Country'.

The armed forces are much diminished now, but the military is not the only army whose loyalty the Queen commands. She and her family also lead large numbers of charity workers and volunteers. This important aspect of their work is a demonstration of what is sometimes called the 'welfare monarchy'. It is not new: since the reign of George III the royal family has become increasingly identified with charity and philanthropy. At the end of the eighteenth century it patronized 90 institutions. By Victoria's death the number was 1,200. Now members of the family head 3,500 different charities and philanthropic bodies. As a result, Britain has one of the most productive voluntary sectors in the world. Frank Prochaska, author of *Royal Bounty*, says the monarchy 'provides a sort of buffer between the central state and society. If you got rid of the monarchy, that would simply reinforce the state monolith.'

The Queen constantly promotes and encourages voluntary work. In 1973 she highlighted the 'many people of all ages who go out to help the old and the lonely, the sick and the handicapped'. She felt their role gave them 'real happiness'. In 1980 she said 'a word of thanks' to those who 'are making a real contribution to their community', whether it be in their job or 'through voluntary organizations or simply their own individual initiative'. She is eager to thank the 'millions of people' who 'give their time, unpaid and usually unsung, to the community, and indeed to those most at risk of exclusion from it'. She feels that such people and their voluntary organizations 'provide the bridges across which the generations travel, meet and learn from one another', give us 'our sense of belonging…help define our sense of duty' and 'keep the nation's heartbeat strong and steady too'.

The monarchy should also be the focus at times of national disaster. Before her coronation, the Queen travelled to the east coast of England to offer comfort to victims of the North Sea floods. In October 1966 a slagheap collapsed onto the mining village of Aberfan in South Wales, killing 146 people, mostly children in their school. The Prime Minister, the Duke of Edinburgh and Lord Snowdon went at once to the scene of the tragedy. The Queen waited, and was criticized for doing so. When she did go, she climbed over the desolate, buried school and talked openly to many of those who had lost children or other relatives. Surrounded by villagers dressed in black, she had tears in her eyes. 'As a mother,' she said, 'I'm trying to understand what your feelings must be. I'm sorry I can give you nothing at present but sympathy.' The villagers were clearly touched. She and Prince Philip had tea with the Williams family, who had lost seven relatives. 'She was very upset,' said Mrs Williams.

Almost 30 years later, in a more cynical time, that same intangible power was still apparent when she went to Dunblane in Scotland, after an intruder had massacred children in their school. Political leaders had already come, decently enough, but it was only the Queen who, above and beyond the political fray, was awaited with anticipation and who could dispense some relief. 'Where is your crown?' one child at Dunblane asked. 'I left it behind; there was no room on the plane,' she answered, lightening the grief in which she so clearly shared.

Harold Wilson – or 'the fourteenth Mr Wilson' as Alec Douglas-Home called him in an ironic riposte to Wilson's mockery that he was 'the fourteenth Earl of Home' – was in many ways the personification of the changing 1960s.

Somewhat to the surprise of the staff at Buckingham Palace, Wilson arrived for the formal 'kissing of hands' on his appointment as Prime Minister with his wife Mary, their two sons, his father and his Political Secretary, Marcia Falkender. Wilson discovered that there was no actual kissing of hands. The

People look to the monarchy for comfort in times of national disaster. In October 1966 the Queen visited Aberfan in Wales after a slagheap collapsed and killed 146 people, mostly children. She was visibly moved, as she was nearly 30 years later, when she laid a wreath at Dunblane after 16 children and a teacher were murdered in their school.

Queen merely asked him if he could form an administration despite the small size of his majority. He replied that he was sure he could.

Wilson was the first of the Queen's prime ministers to be more middle than upper class, the first not to have gone to private school and to have no connection with grouse moors. She quickly came to like him. He did not revere her in the same way that Churchill had done, but he appreciated her and looked forward to his Tuesday meetings. He loved to gossip with her and made sure that the world knew that they got on famously. He fed his staff occasional titbits; his Press Secretary, Joe Haines, later said Wilson told him the Queen had asked about President Giscard d'Estaing's apparent night-time prowling of Paris in search of nubile talent.

Wilson was impressed by the Queen's knowledge and astonishing memory. Indeed, he was appalled to be caught out by her during one of his first weekly meetings when she asked him about a subject on which he had not been briefed. From then on, every week he sent the Queen's Private Secretary a short list of the subjects he wanted to discuss, and he asked to be told in advance of anything she wished to raise.

Surrounded by jealous colleagues, Wilson came to see the Queen as the only senior official with whom he could discuss his problems without fearing that he was handing over a knife to be plunged in his back. According to Haines, he always thought the Queen's advice worth having. Unlike a politician, 'she could take a strategic view. She would question rather than advise. Harold always thought he had to justify any proposals to her, which was good discipline. It meant he had to have his arguments very clear in his own mind because the Queen would pick up if he hadn't done his homework.'

Wilson also appreciated the business of monarchy. He loved pageantry. 'I have a great respect for tradition,' he once said. 'I like the real ceremonies of the monarchy…the Opening of Parliament, the coronation. All that.' He understood what the Queen had to do and how she did it. Some of his more radical ministers were less certain. The first meeting the Queen had with her new Labour Privy Council was memorable. Some ministers were determined to show their disapproval for what they saw as a feudal and antiquated ceremony.

Prime Minister Harold Wilson welcoming the Queen home after her historic
visit to West Germany in 1965.

Tony Benn claims he did 'the most miniature bow ever seen' and 'left
the Palace boiling with indignation, and feeling that this was an attempt to
impose tribal magic and personal loyalty on people whose real duty was only
to their electors'.

Barbara Castle, another of the Queen's more left-wing new ministers,
described the difficulty of walking backwards after she had sworn the Oath of
Allegiance. 'The Queen was very charming. She said, "I've never seen so many
people walk backwards so beautifully. Poor Mrs Castle had so far to go."' Castle
says, 'That endeared her to me because it was a natural charm and it showed a
sense of humour.' Richard Crossman, one of the more intellectual members of
the Wilson government, was bored by what he saw as the pomp of the Court.
But he liked the Queen. 'She puts one at ease immediately…has a lovely
laugh…is a really very spontaneous person.'

Tony Benn, then the Postmaster General, was all for cutting back the monarchy's role in every way possible. He decided that he would strike a blow for democracy and good design by removing the Queen from stamps. Britain is the only country that does not have its name on its stamps. The sovereign's head has always been accepted by the International Postal Union as adequate national identification. If Benn's proposal had been adopted, the stamps would have had to be marked 'Great Britain'. He faced a barrage of hostility from his officials, and decided to try and sort the matter out with the Queen herself. Wilson agreed that he could meet her. The Queen bade him sit down and allowed him to explain the stamps at length. Finally, Benn got to the crux of the problem. He said that the real difficulty was that, up to now, it had been understood in the Post Office that by the Queen's personal command, stamps that did not embody her head could not even be submitted for consideration.

'The Queen was clearly embarrassed and indicated that she had no personal feelings about it at all,' Benn said. He was encouraged when she asked to see the new designs, so he spread them out on the floor, knelt beside them and passed them up to her one at a time. He thought she was sympathetic and left the Palace 'feeling absolutely on top of the world' about an audience that 'had lasted about forty minutes instead of the expected fifteen'. He also thought that the Queen herself was open to change; the problem was 'the forces of reaction' which included 'Palace flunkies and courtiers'. Benn's headless stamps did not see the light of day; he was advised by Number 10 to drop the matter.

Benn noted, rather to his surprise, that Prince Philip had thought a good deal about the monarchy and Britain's place in the world. The Prince said that the Queen's role in government should be simplified. He thought that as people became richer they would show less interest in the monarchy.

Prince Philip was right that the mood was changing. The 1960s saw a concerted and remarkably successful assault upon the structures of cultural traditionalism, including Christian observance. As the poet Philip Larkin famously wrote, 'Sexual intercourse began in nineteen sixty-three... Between the end of the *Chatterley* ban and the Beatles' first LP.'

Beginning with *Love Me Do*, the Beatles were the Pied Pipers of the new age,

The Beatles benefited from Harold Wilson's decision to broaden the honours lists. The police had to restrain a crowd of excited fans at Buckingham Palace when the pop stars came to receive their MBEs.

with its pop concerts, pop records, pop magazines, pop art, pirate radio stations, new fashions, including the mini-skirt, and recreational drugs, all of which, in the words on one writer, 'combined to create an integrated cultural system that swept through the young people of Britain'. It was a lot of fun, but by the end of the 1960s the Beatles were singing about drugs, nihilism and leaving home.

Wilson saw himself as representing this new culture. He extended the honours system to include pop stars, journalists, sportsmen and social workers. There were howls of protest when the Beatles were given MBEs. Tony Benn wrote, 'No doubt Harold did this to be popular and I expect it *was* popular – though it may have been unpopular to some people too.' He further asserted, 'The plain truth is that the Beatles have done more for the royal family by accepting MBEs than the royal family has done for the Beatles by giving them.'

The 1960s also saw the Lord Chamberlain, the head of the Queen's household, relieved of one his more tiresome functions – that of censoring plays. As a result, musicals such as *Hair,* with a mixed-sex chorus standing completely nude before the audience, could actually be staged in 1967. Princess Anne famously went to see it.

The Wilson government embarked on more radical social legislation than any before it. The age of voting was lowered to 18, the Sexual Offences Act permitted homosexual acts between consenting adults over the age of 21, and the Abortion Act in effect legalized abortion. Sexuality was discussed and explored more openly than ever before. Along with access to the birth control pill, these liberalizing measures would have a huge impact on society in the decades ahead.

Television was ambiguous: it straddled both the establishment and the new swinging world. Pop programmes such as *Ready Steady Go* and *Top of the Pops* fed swinging London to the nation, while *That Was The Week That Was* and then *Monty Python's Flying Circus* ridiculed 'establishment' values, British pomposity and the armed forces. Throughout the decade, television became more and more powerful (colour arrived in 1968), and pop music continued as the single greatest harbinger of change.

Many Christian congregations tried to compromise with the new age of youth in the late 1960s by adopting guitars, penny whistles, modern dress, discos and a happy-clappy atmosphere. But such experiments often ended unhappily, with congregations unable to countenance the increasing loudness of the music, the visits of the police and, above all, the brazen nature of teenagers' casual sexual relations. As Callum Brown has shown in *The Death of Christian Britain*, 190 years after Sunday schools first opened, the Church was becoming increasingly irrelevant to an entire generation of youngsters who no longer subscribed to orthodox Christian morality.

The British educational system was also radically changed. The 1960s saw the creation of eight new universities, but students took to sociology more than science and engineering as hoped. For decades, grammar schools had helped gifted working-class children beyond measure but Tony Crosland, Wilson's Education Secretary, said he was going to destroy 'every f***ing grammar school in the country'. Comprehensive schools, less exclusive and less academic, were promoted instead. The curriculum also changed, and instead of being taught the basics, children were encouraged to 'experience'. By the 1970s, Roy Strong points out in *The Story of Britain*, literacy and numeracy were on the decline.

In the face of economic pressures, the government cut back on Britain's military commitments abroad; the last outposts of the Empire were closed and

British troops left Malaya, Aden and finally Singapore. By the 1970s Britain more than ever depended upon the USA for its defence.

The Palace knew that this battery of changes in the country would affect the monarchy. The Duke of Edinburgh said in 1968, 'The monarchy is part of the fabric of the country. And, as the fabric alters, so the monarchy and its people's relations to it alters.' Nevertheless, despite all the changes, and despite criticisms from some, the Queen clearly retained her popularity through the 1960s.

At the end of the decade one of the Queen's private secretaries argued that it was a pity that she could not have closer contact with people than waving from inside a car. Others felt the same. Before the 1970 royal tour, the New Zealand government made clear that it wanted a more relaxed approach. As a result, the so-called 'walkabout' was devised. As they approached Wellington Town Hall, the Queen and Prince Philip got out of their car and strolled along the road greeting the crowds of well-wishers. It must have been nerve racking, not least for their bodyguards, but it was rapturously welcomed in Wellington.

The experiment was repeated in Australia. People were thrilled to get close and speak to the Queen. The *Sydney Morning Herald* declared that the success of the tour 'has surprised the optimists and staggered the pessimists. No more will they [the royal family] appear remote figures removed from reality…they have been seen as warm and human…'

The first British 'walkabout' took place in Coventry in June 1970. Its impact was immense, giving people access to the Queen in a way that would not have been dreamed about in previous reigns. Betty Brown, from Newcastle, had seen the Queen a number of times, but when the Queen stopped to talk to her and accept her flowers, she was enthralled: 'The joy of it all was just so vast, you couldn't explain it.'

William Heseltine is convinced that there were three other important factors that enabled the Queen to remain in touch with social change. The first was Prince Philip, who was always a part of the outside world. The second was television, which allowed the Queen to see and hear things that she would never be shown on official tours. The third was her extraordinary good health. She was rarely ill and never seemed to tire.

But if views from the Palace were broadening, finances were tightening. Money for the monarch has always been a matter of contention in the House of Commons. Parliament first undertook responsibility for the expenses of the royal household after the Revolution of 1688. Since 1760 every monarch has agreed to surrender the income from the Crown estates to Parliament, and in return Parliament gives the monarch an annual provision known as the Civil List. The amount used to be agreed at the start of each reign, and was supposed to remain fixed thereafter.

By the end of the 1960s inflation had taken its toll on the Civil List, which was fixed for the Queen in 1952. Money was becoming tighter and tighter at Buckingham Palace, where salaries were notoriously low. In 1969, Prince Philip gave a television interview in North America in which he warned that the royal family would soon go into the red. 'We may have to move to smaller premises, who knows?' he said.

The Queen on an early royal 'walkabout' during her tour of Australia in 1970. The Australian people were delighted to get so close to her, and 'walkabouts' became a popular feature of her appearances thereafter.

The request for more money aroused hostility in newspapers and Parliament. Wilson performed a valuable service for the Queen when he tackled the Civil List in 1970. In the run-up to an election he could not afford to be seen as anti-monarchist. However, he was also trying to push legislation through Parliament on prices and incomes that would impose restrictions on ordinary workers, so he could not afford to be seen being too generous to the monarchy either. Moreover, he had members of his Cabinet, as well as the parliamentary party, who wanted a thorough investigation into the Queen's personal wealth before the monarchy was given any more state funding.

To avoid making the Civil List a political issue, Wilson agreed with the leader of the opposition Conservative Party, Edward Heath, that a select committee would be formed by whoever came into government after the next election to review the royal finances. Heath won the June 1970 election, and the committee, under the chairmanship of the Chancellor of the Exchequer, Anthony Barber, began its deliberations in May 1971. It contained an avowed republican, William Hamilton, and was quite aggressive in its investigations. The Queen's Private Secretary, Sir Michael Adeane, was called upon to define her official duties. The costs of the royal yacht, the royal train and other perquisites were examined minutely.

The Queen was relieved when Barber announced that details of her personal wealth would remain confidential, but that did not stop press speculation. Huge and inflated totals were bandied around – and editorials criticized the fact that she did not pay tax. The ultimate outcome was the Civil List Act of 1972, which authorized a rise from £475,000 to £980,000 to cover the Queen's expenses and rises for other members of the family. The sum was set for a 10-year period.

The Queen's Tuesday meetings with Edward Heath are not thought to have had the same enjoyably relaxed atmosphere as those with Harold Wilson. Nonetheless, Heath valued her assistance and experience. He said, 'I could make sure that Her Majesty knew what we were doing as a government, what I intended to do as prime minister, and the effect I thought it would have. She expressed her views, which of course were based on great experience…'

One of Heath's principal ambitions was for Britain to join the European Economic Community (EEC), from which France's president, General de Gaulle, had barred the country in the 1960s. Britain's relationship with Europe has always had an effect on the national psyche, even now. Roy Strong argues that 'for five centuries Britain had only involved itself with Europe to defeat any power which threatened to dominate it. After achieving that objective it had then always retreated behind its watery frontiers.'

In 1957 Britain had feared that the Commonwealth would be threatened by entry into the EEC and had instead created the European Free Trade Association (EFTA) with Denmark, Sweden, Portugal and Austria. By 1961 Macmillan thought Britain should join the EEC. The British application was humiliatingly rejected by de Gaulle in January 1963 and again in 1967. In 1970 Heath applied for a third time and, with de Gaulle gone, Britain was accepted. The decision whether to join was put to a free vote in the Commons and passed in July 1972; the country officially entered on 1 January 1973. Over the following years, the new supra-national structures have had important implications for all British institutions, including the monarchy. The overall effect has been to diminish sovereignty.

The Queen's initial concern about Europe was the impact it would have on the Commonwealth. She was determined to reassure its members that they were not being abandoned. In her 1972 Christmas broadcast she stated, 'The new links with Europe will not replace those with the Commonwealth. They cannot alter our historical and personal attachments with kinsmen and friends overseas. Old friends will not be lost.' She embarked on a series of tours in 1973 to reinforce this message.

The young prime minister of Canada, Pierre Trudeau, and his glamorous wife, Margaret, were political stars. He believed that it was time for Canada to have its own head of state. The Queen set out to charm him to stay in the Commonwealth, and succeeded. One member of her household recalls that she was almost flirtatious. 'She was given a parka with hood by the eskimos and she looked gorgeous in it – as she well knew. Trudeau was entranced.'

He was also astonished by the impact that she had, remarking to her Private Secretary that although he and his wife attracted crowds, he had never seen anything like those that rushed to meet the royal couple. Trudeau changed his mind on the desirability of the republican alternative and said, 'The relationship with the Crown has brought much benefit to the people of Canada and will continue to do so; why change it?'

The trip to Australia in October 1973 was also successful. The Queen had gone there to sign the new Royal Styles and Titles Bill brought in by the Labor government of Gough Whitlam. The Queen would no longer be 'Queen of the United Kingdom and of Her Other Realms and Territories' but simply 'Queen of Australia'. She returned to the Pacific in February 1974, but this time her tour was interrupted by Edward Heath's decision to call an election. She had to fly back to London in time for polling day so that she would be ready to receive the Prime Minister, whoever that might be.

Heath's premiership had not been a happy one. This period saw the beginning of the Troubles in Northern Ireland. After Ireland became a republic and left the Commonwealth in 1949, the Attlee government passed the Ireland Act, which stated that Northern Ireland would remain a part of the United Kingdom so long as its population wished it. The Protestants outnumbered the Catholics by two to one, and the Catholics remained in effect an underclass. In 1967 the Civil Rights Association was formed in Northern Ireland, and carried out a series of non-violent demonstrations on behalf of the Catholics. When a march was banned in 1968, there were violent demonstrations in the streets of Londonderry, and next year British troops were sent in to protect the Catholics. Sections of the Catholic Irish Republican Army vowed that the troops were not protectors but the enemy, to be driven out. Protestant paramilitary groups sprang up.

In 1971 the first British soldier was killed in Northern Ireland. Martin Charteris, now the Queen's Private Secretary, suggested that she send the soldier's family a letter of condolence. She declined, on the grounds that it might create a precedent that could not be sustained. In July the situation in Ulster deteriorated as, in Edward Heath's words, 'the IRA stepped up its vicious campaign of violence'. Heath recalls, 'The Queen received me at one of my regular audiences after she had been watching the coverage of riots in Belfast on the television, and was obviously shaken by the ferocity of the events in a part of her

Kingdom. In particular, she was horrified by the film of women's faces contorted with hate as they clung to the high wired fences protecting British troops.' Heath concluded, 'Whenever the Queen is accused of remoteness or indifference towards the tribulations of her subjects, I think back to that moment.'

Health also faced serious economic difficulties. In 1971, some 13 million days were lost in strikes. He tried to limit union power with the Industrial Relations Act of 1971, but the unions refused to abide by the new law. The country's problems were dramatically worsened by the first massive oil price rises of 1973. In the face of energy shortages, Heath put the country on a three-day week and struggled for months with strikes by the coal miners. Share prices fell by 70 per cent in 30 months, inflation soared, and the February 1974 election was fought around the question 'Who governs Britain?' Unfortunately for Heath, a majority thought it should not be him. The Conservatives won 297 seats to Labour's 301; there were 14 Liberals and nine Scottish and Welsh nationalists. The result presented the Palace with a potential constitutional problem. If no one could form a majority

In August 1969, British troops were sent to Northern Ireland as the province threatened to descend into serious disorder.

in the Commons, the Queen's prerogative would come into play and she would
have to choose someone to form an administration. Over several days Heath
tried to negotiate an agreement with the Liberals that would enable him to stay
in office. He failed, and informed the Queen. She sent once more for Harold
Wilson, who became Prime Minister for a second time. He won a third victory in
October 1974 with a narrow overall majority of three. Heath was subsequently
replaced by Margaret Thatcher as leader of the Conservative Party.

The country's economic crisis worsened during Wilson's premiership. In 1975
inflation rose to 25 per cent. This caused a new Civil List crisis: once again, the
Palace appeared to be running out of money. Harold Wilson handled the request
for a rise from £980,000 to £1,400,000 with characteristic sympathy. In an angry
parliamentary debate on the Civil List bill, Enoch Powell, a controversial politician but probably the House's greatest parliamentarian, made a remarkable
speech on the Crown and the constitution in his stern, gravelly voice. He insisted
that the Crown is part of the birthright of every citizen of the United Kingdom.
Kenneth Stowe, Wilson's Private Secretary, recalled that Wilson listened intently
and then 'scuttled along the benches to me where I was sitting in the official box,
leaned over and said, "I wish I could have made a speech like that." '

There were those in the Labour Party who thought that their prime minister
was becoming too cosy with the monarchy. The Civil List request was given
more publicity by a new book, *My Queen and I,* by Willie Hamilton, the republican
Labour MP. After an angry debate, a bill allowing the Treasury to adjust the Civil
List for inflation was passed, but not before a significant minority of Labour MPs
had made their opposition very clear.

Meanwhile, there were problems in Australia. The role of the monarch was
being debated in one of Britain's oldest dominions. In 1975 the country witnessed
fierce domestic political dispute. The Labor government of Gough Whitlam
was in chaos. The opposition under Malcolm Fraser blocked the passage of the
government's budget in the Senate, and the government was about to run out of
money. Whitlam refused to call a general election. The Governor-General Sir
John Kerr decided that it was his duty to break the deadlock. On 11 November he
sacked Gough Whitlam as prime minister, and immediately installed Malcolm

Fraser as caretaker, with the agreement that he would pass the budget, not propose any new legislation and call an immediate general election. Kerr did all this under the authority of the Crown.

There was a massive row about Kerr's use of the prerogative powers. Correctly, he had not told Buckingham Palace what he planned to do because he did not want to involve the Queen in the dispute. There were angry demonstrations and the crisis called the whole issue of the Australian monarchy into question, fuelling republican sentiment. Fraser won the forthcoming election overwhelmingly, but Kerr was never forgiven by the left, and his controversial action ruined him.

Back home in March 1976, Harold Wilson stunned the country by announcing that he planned to resign. His second term had not been a great success: the government was still dominated by a collectivist ideology that was ill equipped to deal with the current economic crises.

Wilson's departure provoked speculation and innuendo for years to come, but, according to Wilson's own account, there was nothing sudden in his decision – he had informed the Queen at Balmoral in September 1975. She had driven Wilson and his wife, Mary, to a log cabin on the estate, where they had tea. While the Queen and Mary Wilson washed up, Wilson told her that he intended to resign in six months' time. This was then confirmed with Martin Charteris, the Queen's Private Secretary, and again in a weekly audience with the Queen on 9 December.

Wilson's resignation honours list was another source of gossip. It contained names that his critics considered unsuitable. When it was placed before her, the Queen apparently raised her eyes at one of the beneficiaries of the Prime Minister's bounty and said to her Private Secretary, 'Please remind the Prime Minister there is always time to think again.' On this occasion the Prime Minister did not take his monarch's advice.

The Queen was nonetheless concerned that he should leave his office with dignity. Kenneth Stowe and Martin Charteris discussed how the resignation should be handled with appropriate ceremony. They decided that, like Churchill, Wilson should invite the Queen to dinner at Number 10. According to Stowe, 'this idea was obviously approved by the Queen'. Wilson, taken aback at first, was

Martin Charteris, the Queen's Assistant Private Secretary and later Private Secretary, inspired all those who worked with him. Here he is seen discussing state papers with the Queen on board *Britannia*.

immensely flattered. The dinner was a great success and the Queen raised a laugh when she remarked in her speech that it was nice for the two tenants of the tied cottages at either end of The Mall to get together.

The parliamentary Labour Party elected James Callaghan to succeed Wilson, and the Queen duly sent for him as leader of the largest party in the House. Callaghan recorded in his memoirs, 'Audrey and I left the moment I received the summons and drove to the Palace together. There she waited in an ante-room while the Queen received me in audience and invited me to form a government.' This was a necessary step to conform with the well-established convention that when the Prime Minister resigns, the government ceases to exist. 'There is no formal ceremony for the appointment of a prime minister. That evening I took no oath and received no official communication.'

Like Wilson, Callaghan enjoyed his Tuesday meetings with the Queen. They developed a good relationship. One of his officials recollects that 'On one occasion, the Queen took him for a walk round the garden at Buckingham Palace for the audience, and she picked some lily of the valley and put them in his buttonhole. As we went back to Number 10, he was obviously vastly impressed and very pleased, and made sure that I knew all about it.'

When new governments are formed the Queen has to swear in the new, but also say farewell to outgoing ministers. One who did not survive Callaghan's reshuffle was Barbara Castle, who remarked that 'the Queen is extremely professional…she would be genned up on everybody; she used to do her homework, and she used to take these functions extremely seriously.' Castle reflects that the Queen was able to 'discharge her duties with sensitivity and the knowledge of what was required of her. She chatted for a bit perfectly naturally and then said, "Well, Mrs Castle, I want to thank you for all you've done while you've been a minister," because I had been four different ministers.'

Roy Hattersley, a republican, recalls his leave-taking of the Queen. 'She asked me what it had been like; I said it had been great but there had been moments where I'd been nervous about what was happening… She was very interested in what happened when I felt nervous. Did I feel so nervous that I wanted to give it up? Did I feel so nervous that I'd had to consult other colleagues? And there was a feeling that she was actually interested in the machinery of government. We sat down, one to one, and had a perfectly serious conversation…'

The Queen's Silver Jubilee year, 1977, dawned grimly. The economy had almost never been in worse shape. Inflation and unemployment were roaring upwards; the unions seemed all powerful. The fundamental truth was that none of the Queen's governments in the last 25 years had been able to deal successfully with the country's problems. The Callaghan government now had to apply to the International Monetary Fund for a loan that was granted only in return for large cuts in public expenditure. There was an abiding sense of failure in both Westminster and the country.

Both the government and the Queen were concerned about how extensively and expensively the Jubilee should be celebrated. But Martin Charteris and other Palace officials felt there was clearly a need to celebrate 25 years of the Queen's reign. According to her Press Secretary, Ronald Allison, 'soundings… were taken throughout the Commonwealth, particularly the Commonwealth

The Queen talking to well-wishers in Camberwell, south London, during the Silver Jubilee celebrations. Events took place throughout the year, climaxing on 7 June.

monarchies', and they 'brought back the same sort of response'. So an ambitious programme was drawn up, which eventually took the Queen to every part of the United Kingdom, including Northern Ireland, and to all the Commonwealth monarchies.

Momentum built throughout the year, beginning with a tour of the Pacific, Western Samoa, Tonga, Fiji, New Zealand, Australia and Papua New Guinea. Later in the year she also went to Canada and the Caribbean. The welcome was tremendous – thousands upon thousands turned out for her everywhere. Commodore Anthony Morrow, who was on board *Britannia* (the yacht that he was later to command) during 1977, remembers, 'Everywhere we went, we had these aquatic welcomes: boats, people – harbour entrances would be just packed with people everywhere.'

As the year went on, more and more people throughout Britain began to gather to express their affection for and appreciation of the Queen. Street parties were organized: there were 4,000 in London alone and thousands more across the country. The numbers who turned out to greet her or celebrate ran into the millions.

The high point of the celebrations took place in London on 7 June, when the Queen went to St Paul's Cathedral for a Thanksgiving Service. The Gold Coach, used for her coronation, was re-leafed. The coachmen and horses had to practise

At a time of recession, the street parties held all over the country to celebrate the Silver Jubilee lifted the national mood.

by towing around Hyde Park an old army vehicle filled with sand to match the four-ton weight of the coach. Nothing, however, could prepare them for the actual day. One coachman, Stephen Matthews, remembers being a confident young man at the time. 'I wasn't over-stressed or worried about it until the evening before when I took my dogs for a walk. In front of the Palace I saw rows of people up each side of The Mall. They were all camped out, singing, Primus stoves going. And then I thought, crikey, if something goes wrong tomorrow, I'm in trouble. And that's when I got nervous.'

A million people filled The Mall. 'We went out the gates and we were just met by this almighty roar,' says Alfred Oates, another coachman. 'It was just one noise, from the moment we went outside the gate till you actually got to St Paul's, and your ears were ringing…you just couldn't hear anything.' Matthews remembers, 'You couldn't even hear the horses' feet hitting the floor.' There were 'banks of people each side of the road', and 'the people were of very, very mixed ages…ninety, right down to toddlers'. He adds, 'One young lad, I suppose mid-teens, was halfway up a lamppost, waving a banner with Queen on it – obviously he'd been to a rock concert recently.'

Not all tributes were as reverent. The unruly punk rock group the Sex Pistols released the single 'God Save the Queen', which referred to the Queen as 'a moron'. It was banned by the BBC – the controller of Radio One said it was 'in gross bad taste' – and some shops refused to sell it. Despite that, it topped the charts. But everywhere the Queen went she was greeted with thunderous applause. When she drove through Nottingham, Ronald Allison remembers, 'As far as you could see there were just thousands and thousands of people waiting. Wherever she went the crowds loved her; people just sort of parted, and she walked through unmolested, and was handed Mars bars and little bouquets picked from the local park a couple of minutes earlier.' Her deputy chauffeur at the time, Ted Harrison, says, 'You could tell how welcome she was by the amount of flowers given to her. We used to carry them in the boot of the Rolls, but every hour or so we had to remove them, or we'd never have got them all in.' The flowers were sent to hospitals and schools. The ladies-in-waiting collected any tabs with names and addresses to write thank-you letters afterwards.

The huge crowds that thronged The Mall in front of Buckingham Palace recalled the enthusiasm felt at the time of the coronation in 1953.

The Labour leadership was astonished. Those who supported the Queen, like Callaghan, were delighted and basked in her reflected glory. The republicans in the party were dismayed.

At the Guildhall lunch held in her honour on 7 June, she poignantly recalled the promise she had made in South Africa many years earlier: 'When I was 21,' she said, 'I pledged my life to the service of our people and I asked for God's help to make good that vow. Although that vow was made in my salad days when I was green in judgement, I do not regret or retract one word of it.' She sat down to great applause.

'She had a love affair with the country,' said Martin Charteris, who, to the sorrow of the Queen and himself, stood down as private secretary soon after the Jubilee. She was genuinely touched by it all. 'I am simply amazed, I had no idea,' one courtier remembers her saying over and over again. Another person close to the Queen recalls her asking in disbelief, 'Why me? I'm just an ordinary person.' Princess Margaret said later that she had to push her sister out on to the balcony at Buckingham Palace, to be cheered again and again by the crowds singing 'Land of Hope and Glory'.

The events of the year showed clearly that the monarchy was still, to use the Queen's phrase from 1954, 'living in the hearts of the people'.

five

Women at Work

In the spring of 1979 Nicholas Henderson, one of Britain's most thoughtful ambassadors, retired from the Foreign Office and sent a final dispatch in which he bemoaned Britain's decline. He said that the rest of the world thought Britain had squandered its power. He was right.

At the beginning of the Queen's reign, Britain was the strongest economic and military power in Europe and the leader in atomic energy. In 1979 we were no longer even in the front rank of European powers. GNP per capita, percentage of world trade and productivity – all such indicators showed us trailing France and Germany. Our industrial relations were far worse than theirs: in 1977 we lost 10 million working days to strikes, while France lost 2.5 million and Germany under 160,000. Management was inefficient, but, Henderson asked, what incentive was there when top executives were taxed at over 80 per cent and faced closed shops and a process of arbitration that the unions usually won?

His dispatch chimed with everyday realities. Everything about Britain seemed to be getting worse. In the face of inflation and the unions, the government appeared inept. The winter of 1978–9 brought a series of strikes by road transport workers, ambulance drivers, gravediggers, dustmen and others. There was no one to dispose of the bodies or rubbish. The reality was awful, and its impact was real and disagreeable. It was such a clear reversal of the rising standards of living which every government had promised and which voters expected, that the period became known as 'the winter of discontent'.

When the Scottish nationalists removed their support from the Labour government, the Conservative leader, Margaret Thatcher, called for a vote of confidence, which the government lost. Callaghan drove to Buckingham Palace

◁ Margaret Thatcher saw herself as both a radical prime minister and an intensely loyal subject of the Queen.

The sight of uncollected rubbish was a potent symbol of the 'winter of discontent' of 1978–9. It hastened the end of the Labour government.

to tender his resignation to the Queen, and an election was held in May 1979. The Conservatives won power, having spent 11 of the previous 15 years in opposition. It was a historic moment. For the first time in her reign, the Queen invited a woman to form a government. Mrs Thatcher accepted, becoming Britain's first female prime minister. Not much was ever the same again.

Margaret Thatcher vividly remembers the first time she was called to the Palace by the Queen. 'I went and sat in Central Office waiting for the call to come,' she told me. 'Just waiting, conscious of the enormity of what I was likely to be asked to do. And it all comes in on you at that particular moment, the responsibility.'

She said that the Queen 'always knows exactly what to do. She always knows how to put you at your ease.' She said, 'I knew that if I didn't do well as a woman prime minister, there wouldn't be another.' Thatcher was adamant that their shared gender was irrelevant to their relationship: 'The Queen was the monarch and it happens that she was a perfect lady. I was a prime minister; it happened that I was a woman. But it was the monarch talking to the Prime Minister, and therefore it was the same constitutional relationship as any monarch talking to any prime minister.'

There was much speculation about how these two women would get on; until now each had been the most powerful woman in her own overwhelmingly male environment. Now each had another strong woman to deal with.

The Queen's methods are gentle, almost oblique, but they are nonetheless clear. One of Mrs Thatcher's ministers once said that being shouted down by Mrs Thatcher was very unpleasant, 'but I'd much rather have that than take the Queen's disapproval. I just wouldn't want to take those eyes and those folded arms.'

Mrs Thatcher was determined and radical but, paradoxically, she was probably the 'most obedient servant' amongst all the Queen's prime ministers. She had grown up as a strict monarchist in the house of her alderman father. Like millions of others, the family's Christmas lunch was timed to listen to the Queen's Christmas broadcast at 3 p.m. – that was as important as going to church on Christmas morning.

Thatcher told me many years later about her recollections of the sad photographs of King George VI saying farewell to his daughter at London airport just before he died. It was clear just how ill he was, she said: 'He just stood at the end of the runway and waved goodbye to the aircraft. He had dark, deep circles under his eyes. And that shot of him is so compelling that it has remained with me ever since.' She mourned the King. This eager young Conservative politician was also an early feminist, writing in a newspaper article at the time, 'If, as many earnestly pray, the accession of Elizabeth II can help to remove the last shreds of prejudice against women aspiring to the highest places, then a new era for women will indeed be at hand.' On coronation day, she recalled, she and her husband Denis 'splashed out' on seats in Parliament Square to watch the procession pass by.

Thatcher was in awe of the Queen, both of her person and position. She was determined to show her loyalty: she would curtsy lower than almost anyone. She used to arrive for her Tuesday meetings 15 minutes early, to guarantee that she would not be late. Once she was too early for the Prime Minister's annual visit at Balmoral, so she and her staff paced up and down a remote Scottish roadside until it was time to arrive.

Thatcher was determined to overturn the domestic consensus, which favoured the industrial and social compromise the major parties had endorsed since 1945. She was correct that radical treatment was needed to arrest Britain's apparently inexorable decline. She believed that the country could not afford a full-employment economy and a welfare state. Her solution was to forswear the ambition of full employment, allow inefficient industries and companies to go to the wall and, in the process, destroy the power of the unions. She famously insisted 'there is no alternative', and many of her policies were ultimately successful. But they were, as she intended, a painful shock to the system.

Ferdinand Mount, who now worked at 10 Downing Street as what he calls Margaret Thatcher's 'political valet', has written, 'She could be petty, vindictive, obtuse. Like almost all successful politicians, she never shrank from repeating herself. She was a stranger to irony. Yet far outweighing these minor weaknesses, she radiated a sense of possibility. She always believed that something could be done. And she was determined to see that it was done, if necessary – in fact preferably – by herself alone... This can-do attitude, as the Americans call it, is perhaps her greatest legacy.'

Early on, her zealous reforms were denounced even by some on her own side as 'divisive'; her predecessor, Edward Heath, saw them as a threat to the fabric of British society.

She aroused greater fury on the left, and her attempts to reform union laws led to a series of industrial actions. The most intractable was the 1984–5 miners' strike, which caused violence between police and protesters on a scale rarely seen in Britain. Her ultimate success in reforming union laws and changing the industrial culture helped make Britain more attractive to investors than at any time in recent decades. But there were constant rumours that the Queen found Thatcher's harsh confrontations uncomfortable.

One of the first crises Mrs Thatcher had to deal with concerned the Commonwealth – the attempt to negotiate an end to the illegal, unilateral declaration of Rhodesian independence under the white minority leader Ian Smith, before the fighting between his regime and the black guerrillas caused a wider and bloodier war.

Whatever Mrs Thatcher's views on Rhodesia before she became Prime Minister, she was reluctantly persuaded that a deal between Smith and the guerrillas had to be reached. In August 1979, Commonwealth heads of government were due to meet in Lusaka, capital of Zambia, where many of the guerrillas fighting the Smith regime were based. This was expected to be, at the very least, a bad-tempered meeting, and there was even speculation about the dangers from the guerrillas.

There were rumours that the Queen might be advised by her Prime Minister not to attend. However, she had attended every biennial Commonwealth Heads of Government Meeting since Edward Heath asked her not to go to Singapore in 1971, to prevent her from becoming embroiled in a row about British arms sales to South Africa.

She had always been deeply concerned with Commonwealth matters and had done her utmost to ensure that her position as Head of the Commonwealth was not seen simply as an extension of the position of Queen of the United Kingdom – which would not have been acceptable to other members. In 1979 she thought she had a role to play in Lusaka. Mrs Thatcher did not attempt to dissuade her; as she said to me, 'If the Queen wanted to go, then the Queen had to go, and all the necessary security had to be put in place.'

Lord Carrington, Foreign Secretary from 1979 to 1982, states that 'Thatcher was viewed with a good deal of suspicion by all the Africans, and most of the Asians, and in fact by most of the Commonwealth'. He thought that the meeting at Lusaka had 'all the hallmarks of being very unpleasant, and not to say a disaster', but the Queen 'played an enormous role in calming everything down'.

Lusaka confirmed that in many ways the most important event at any

The Queen's diplomacy helped calm the fractious Commonwealth leaders' meeting in Lusaka in August 1979. This led to agreement on the future of Rhodesia, which became the independent state of Zimbabwe.

Commonwealth summit is the private session the Queen has with each of the leaders. Sir Sonny Ramphal, former Secretary General of the Commonwealth, says, 'You are sitting at this serious conference table and you see a prime minister slipping away. And you know what is happening: he is going off to have his meeting with the Queen. I've known a good many Commonwealth prime ministers and presidents now of various hues and various attitudes to the monarch, and I have never yet encountered one who didn't attach the very greatest importance to those 20 minutes. Many a time they would say to me, "My goodness how much she knows about my country, how well tuned in she is".'

Douglas Hurd, another former Foreign Secretary, agrees. 'She helps to bring them together, and even if they're being bad tempered with each other on particular things, in the evening it's different because they're all guests of the

Queen. She doesn't intervene in discussions or try to resolve disputes, that's not her role as she sees it, but she does provide occasions, events and her own personality, which certainly help to unify.' President Kaunda of Zambia, the host in Lusaka, adds, 'Queen Elizabeth is a human being, first and foremost. Her approach to life is down to earth, very human indeed. That is how she won the love and respect of most of us black nationalists.'

The Queen was concerned that the conference find a solution to the Rhodesia crisis and she apparently suggested that it would be helpful if local newspapers could be constructive rather than merely abusive of the British government. In his biography of the Queen, Kenneth Harris quotes the *Annual Register*, which declared that the heated atmosphere whipped up by the local government newspaper was 'cooled by the presence of Her Majesty the Queen'. The *Register* said she 'could easily be elected Queen of the World'.

Lee Kuan Yew, Prime Minister of Singapore, describes the Queen's presence as having a mollifying effect. 'Margaret Thatcher was not forthcoming about independence for Rhodesia, but there was this mother figure who represented the wider British public and the Commonwealth, who showed a softer side, a more humane side and one that sympathized with these aspirations.' Thatcher concurs, 'It was a very successful conference, and was I glad she was there! Any difficulties were smoothed over really because of her presence and because everyone had an audience with her.'

The Lusaka summit agreed to call an all-party constitutional conference on Rhodesia. This met in September at Lancaster House in London, and the parties signed an agreement under which Rhodesia's Unilateral Declaration of Independence was ended, sanctions were lifted, and Lord Soames went out as interim governor to hold elections. Robert Mugabe, leader of ZANU, one of the strongest groups fighting white rule, was elected President, and in April 1980 the newly named Zimbabwe was granted independence as the forty-third member of the Commonwealth in a ceremony presided over by the Prince of Wales.

Mugabe has subsequently proved to be a disastrous leader, but at the time Lusaka showed that the Commonwealth had an important international role to play. And the Queen's diplomacy demonstrated the truth of her Press

Secretary's claim that her role as Head of the Commonwealth 'is no longer a hangover from colonial days. Instead there has been a spelling-out of a new perception of her role.' The Queen herself said that the saga had demonstrated the Commonwealth's 'uniquely effective system for bringing progress out of conflict'.

The Queen has used her diplomatic skills to ease other changes within the Commonwealth. The Canadian Prime Minister, Pierre Trudeau, had proposed at the end of the 1970s a new constitution that would end Westminster's remaining constitutional role in Canada. This desire for change was fuelled by domestic arguments between the French-speaking minority centred in Quebec, which was fundamentally republican, and the more conservative, monarchist majority. The Queen was caught in the middle, but she was involved in behind-the-scenes discussions on the legislation. All sides concur that she played an important role in helping Canadian politicians find an agreement. In January 1982 the British Parliament passed the new Canada Act, which ended any British executive authority in Canada, while preserving the monarchy there. Trudeau declared, 'The Constitution of Canada has come home.' The functions of the sovereign had now been transferred to the governor-general but, as *The Times* proclaimed, 'The Queen remains Queen of Canada...all the easier for Canadians to accept because she will no longer be burdened by identification with the constitutional issues'. The Queen was delighted.

In April 1982 Argentina invaded the Falkland Islands, one of the last outposts of the British Empire. Parliament was united in its condemnation of this affront to British sovereignty, and Thatcher, struggling in the depths of unpopularity, instructed the Ministry of Defence to muster a task force to seize back the islands.

As the historian Ben Pimlott points out, the Queen was involved in the crisis in four distinct ways: 'as sovereign of the country whose sovereignty had been breached by the invasion, and whose government had declared its intentions of regaining the island; as Head of the Commonwealth and of the remaining fragments of Empire, which included the Falklands; as head of the armed forces; and as mother of a combatant.' Thatcher says, 'I remember going to see the Queen to report about the Falklands and of course to ask whether Prince Andrew [a naval helicopter pilot] should go. I was told very firmly that Prince Andrew had decided he was going. The Queen was obviously very proud. So was I. No question, Prince Andrew was going. And he did go, and of course accredited himself wonderfully.'

The British expedition succeeded in recapturing the islands, providing a huge boost to British morale. In June 1983 Thatcher called an election, which she won with an overwhelming majority. She committed herself to a radical restructuring of the British economy. This included further privatization, union reform, the encouragement of private enterprise and the diminution of the welfare state.

That year there was political turmoil on the Caribbean island of Grenada, a member of the Commonwealth where the Queen was Head of State. Its Prime

Prince Andrew served in the Falklands War as a helicopter pilot. He was in playful mood when he was greeted by his mother on his return, after Britain's victory over Argentina.

Minister was killed in a left-wing coup. Sir Paul Scoon, the Governor-General, asked the Reagan administration for assistance. America invaded and re-established order on the island. Neither the Queen nor her British Prime Minister had been informed of the invasion. Sir Robin Butler, then Thatcher's Private Secretary, remembers, 'I was in Number 10 that night when Margaret Thatcher was trying to get in touch with Ronald Reagan on the hot line. One got the sense that Reagan was not eager to pick up the telephone. But eventually he did. And I must say that he sounded like a naughty boy who thought he was going to get a wigging. His first words were, "I'm afraid it's too late, Margaret, it's too late." '

Thatcher recalls, 'I said [to President Reagan], "They're the Queen's islands."' She was surprised that her friend Reagan had taken such unilateral action: 'I don't think he'd thought it through, although he was devoted to the Queen. His advisers should have told him, "Look, if you want to go in, you simply must get the consent of the Queen and her Prime Minister." I said, "Just remember in future, we are your friends."'

The Queen and Thatcher were united in the face of a dangerous enemy – the IRA. In October 1984 the Queen was on a rare holiday in the United States when the IRA blew up the Grand Hotel in Brighton in an attempt to murder Thatcher, who was attending the Conservative Party Conference there. Five people were killed, and there were many serious casualties. Thatcher was fortunate to escape unhurt. When the Queen heard of the bombing, she was staying with her old friend Lord Carnarvon and his American wife, Jeanie, in their house in Wyoming. Lord Carnarvon remembers being instructed by the Queen's Private Secretary, Philip Moore, that 'the Queen must not speak to anybody on the telephone until she's spoken to the Prime Minister'.

This became a problem. Carnarvon could not reach Thatcher, and his telephone never stopped ringing with President Reagan's Private Secretary asking to speak to the Queen. 'I finally did get through,' he recalled. 'Mrs Thatcher came to the telephone and her first words were, "Are you having a wonderful time?" I thought that was fairly moving, considering what she'd just been through.' The Queen commiserated with Mrs Thatcher, who remembers that the call 'boosted one's morale'. It was only after this that Carnarvon allowed President Reagan's call to be put through to the Queen.

As Thatcher's reforms continued in her second term, there were rumours that her confrontations with those she saw as enemies of Britain led to strains in her relations with the Queen. Charles Powell, Thatcher's principal foreign affairs aide, was aware of 'at least two occasions when there were reports of unease in the Palace about certain policies. One was during the miners' strike, the other was during the row over sanctions against South Africa.'

In 1984 the IRA tried to murder Mrs Thatcher by blowing up the Grand Hotel, Brighton, where she was staying. Five people died and many were injured in one of the worst terrorist outrages on mainland Britain.

The Queen was certainly upset by the miners' strike. She received many letters from miners' families telling her of the hard times they were living through; inevitably she was touched by these. Powell says, 'The monarchy sees itself as steward of the nation as a whole, and attaches great importance to national consensus and social peace. When, during the miners' strike, matters became extremely confrontational, even violent, between the police and the miners, there were reports of concern that the government was pushing things too far, was putting the miners in a corner, was threatening the whole social fabric of the country.' He adds, 'I have no idea whether those were true or not, but they were certainly issuing, let's say, through channels around Buckingham Palace.'

Martin Charteris told me in 1994, long after he had ceased to be the Queen's Private Secretary, 'The Queen probably prefers a sort of consensus politics rather than a polarized one. I suspect this is true, although I can't really speak from knowledge here. If you are in the Queen's position, you are the symbolic head of a country, and the less squabbling that goes on in that country, obviously the more comfortable you feel. Therefore I suspect – and I think it's only natural – that politics which are very polarized are very uncomfortable to the sovereign. I think that must be so.' Mrs Thatcher, by contrast, clearly thought that polarization was essential if problems were to be confronted and dealt with boldly.

Others disagree with this conventional analysis. David Owen, former Labour Foreign Secretary and a founder of the Social Democrat Party, believes the Queen must have been relieved that at last someone was tackling Britain's crippling economic problems. 'I think,' he says, 'she would have understood some of the trade union reforms and economic reforms and some of the hard, rather polarized policies of the eighties were necessary.'

As for the Commonwealth, the Queen and Thatcher did have rather different perspectives. Kenneth Baker, one of Thatcher's own ministers, observed, 'The Queen thought that the Commonwealth meetings were very important events and she spent a lot of time at them, looking upon herself as the mother of a large family. That was not the attitude of Mrs Thatcher. Margaret Thatcher liked

Margaret Thatcher's cures for the country's economic ills were tough; the 1984–5 miners' strike was one of many bitter confrontations between the government and the unions during this period.

the Commonwealth, yes, but she did not like being lectured by a whole lot of African leaders about how she should run her country when she saw them running their countries very badly indeed.' It was certainly true that one of the great disappointments of the Commonwealth was that so many states had evolved not into democracies, but into one-party systems disfigured by dictatorship and corruption.

In the mid-1980s Commonwealth unity was put to the test over the issue of South Africa and sanctions against its apartheid regime. The Queen, as ever, had to be cautious in expressing her views on South Africa. Sir Sonny Ramphal says, 'She didn't come out and make a great speech denouncing apartheid. But it was very clear to everyone, including the government of South Africa, where she stood.' The Queen's attitude towards sanctions was more difficult to gauge. Ramphal says, 'Sanctions were not the clear-cut issue that apartheid was.

There were arguments for and against, and she [the Queen] didn't get herself embroiled in that.' Mrs Thatcher certainly had little sympathy for the African National Congress (ANC), the black nationalist party that she regarded as a terrorist organization. She saw sanctions as both ineffective and unwise. Throughout the 1980s a gulf grew between Britain and many of its Commonwealth partners on the issue.

In 1985 the Commonwealth Conference at Nassau decided, after much argument with Thatcher, that an Eminent Persons Group would be sent to South Africa to advise whether sanctions should be imposed. In 1986 the group came out strongly in favour of sanctions. The hope, in Ramphal's words, was 'to push the South Africans over the edge. That was not the kind of action Mrs Thatcher relished.'

The press speculation that the Queen was privately opposed to Thatcher reached its apogee on 20 July 1986 when *The Sunday Times* published a sensational story alleging an unprecedented rift between the two. The paper claimed that quite apart from differences on the Commonwealth and South Africa, the Queen was concerned about her government's lack of compassion, its handling of the miners' strike and its disregard of the postwar consensus that she thought had served Britain well. Even more extraordinary than the paper's ability to report so confidently on the Queen's views, was its claim that she actually wanted those views to be made public by *The Sunday Times.*

Sir William Heseltine, the Queen's Private Secretary, confirmed in a letter to *The Times* that her Press Secretary, Michael Shea, had talked to a *Sunday Times* journalist several times. But he disputed the remarks as published. The editor of *The Sunday Times,* Andrew Neil, stood by the story. He insisted that Shea had indeed spoken of rifts between the Queen and Thatcher, and that the Palace expected this to be published. But Shea is adamant: 'The story was untrue. Simple as that.'

Thatcher happened to be staying with the Queen at Holyroodhouse in Edinburgh that very weekend. She and her husband Denis were upset by the story. Shea apologized to her. Thatcher was generous to him. At Sunday lunch, Shea said, 'I was plonked between the Queen and the Prime Minister to show that there was no harm done.' But such stories were damaging to Mrs Thatcher. 'She was unhappy about them, not unnaturally,' said Charles Powell. 'Her view was that ordinary people anywhere in the country would say, "That Mrs Thatcher, she's upsetting the Queen. We can't elect her again."'

Whatever Michael Shea may have said to *The Sunday Times*, it beggars belief that the Queen, having observed the strictest constitutional rectitude throughout her life, would suddenly throw caution and good practice to the wind and break the almost sacred bonds of confidentiality with which she and all her prime ministers had treated their relationship.

Soon after *The Sunday Times* story, in August 1986, Commonwealth leaders met again in London to try to find agreement on the sanctions issue. The Queen organized a working dinner. 'I'm not sure there's ever been a working dinner at a Commonwealth Meeting before or since,' said Ramphal. The then Foreign Secretary, Geoffrey Howe, remembers, 'We'd been working all day in circumstances of quite sharp disagreement to try and find a common position. Britain was very much detached from all our colleagues, and the coming together under royal auspices was a very deliberate act by the Queen, I think, to remind us all of our commitment to get on with each other.'

Ramphal believes that for Thatcher, the only leader against sanctions, it 'was a message with strong overtones'. Without her saying anything explicitly, it seemed clear that the Queen desired unity in the Commonwealth, and wanted a resolution over the question of sanctions. Former President Kaunda of Zambia recalls with a laugh that he was talking to the Queen, 'And then she said, "My friend, you and I should be careful, we are under the scrutiny of the British Prime Minister." I looked up and I saw Mrs Thatcher had fixed her eyes on us. I don't know what she thought we were doing. She was looking at us in a very strange way. So I said, "Ma'am, I must leave you."'

Subsequently, the rumour of rift benefited the Foreign Secretary. Geoffrey Howe remembers, 'I was on a mission to Southern Africa, trying to persuade them to abandon apartheid, and was received by Kaunda who was in a pretty tempestuous mood. He told me that he would not have received me simply as a member of the British government because his dancing partner – he'd danced

The relationship between the Queen, to whom consensus is vital, and Mrs Thatcher, who thrived on confrontation, was a subject of much gossip and endless fascination.

with Margaret Thatcher at Lusaka – was now dancing with apartheid. A pretty unkind crack, but that's what he said. But he was prepared to receive me because of his love and respect for Her Majesty the Queen.'

Kaunda confirmed the point: 'I was really very upset by what the British government was doing at that time and so I said I would not receive him. In the end I changed my mind. But I made the point that I was meeting him because of my respect for the Queen, that grand lady who deserved better. I met Howe not because of Margaret Thatcher, but because of the Queen.'

In the end, the Commonwealth did help to end apartheid by bringing the issue to the fore, by encouraging dialogue between South African President de Klerk and the imprisoned black nationalist Nelson Mandela, and by support-ing the transition to democracy. Throughout, the Queen played an important role. David Owen says, 'I very much doubt whether the Commonwealth, going through the strains of South Africa and other strains, would have survived without her as a symbol of continuity and her constant, deeply committed presence. If it matters to her, then it must matter to me, that sort of argument.'

Thatcher pays a similar tribute to the Queen. 'Without Her Majesty's role as Head of the Commonwealth the association wouldn't have its unity. Her role is not a formal role, but it's a very real role, and it's greater in performance than in theory because of the marvellous person she is. She knows how to smooth things over, she knows the right things to say.'

Thatcherism called into question the purpose and viability of many British institutions. It was inevitable that the monarchy was affected. During the 1980s, criticism of royal spending and the Queen's tax-free status increased. The media fuelled the fire, relishing stories of royal extravagance, especially amongst the younger members of the family. The press once again began to speculate about the Queen's private assets, always a closely guarded secret at the Palace. *Fortune* magazine claimed the Queen's personal wealth was £7 billion, increasing at a rate of £3 million a day. The tabloids jumped on such exaggerations, which included assets that the monarch technically owns, but cannot sell, since they are held in trust for the nation. One poll in the *Independent on Sunday* found that 79 per cent of those polled thought the Queen should be taxed.

The Queen authorized a radical restructuring of her household, carried out by Lord Airlie who was appointed Lord Chamberlain (head of the household) in 1984. He was a Scottish aristocrat and shrewd businessman, who had been chairman of the merchant bank Schroders. He had known the Queen all his life. When he arrived at Buckingham Palace he realized that a comprehensive review was needed.

The household had not fundamentally changed since Prince Albert's day. Since that time its remit and responsibilities had decreased. Successive governments had lost faith in the household's ability to manage its own affairs and had taken over many of its functions, such as the maintenance of palaces and royal transport. These changes might have helped to conceal costs, but they had diminished the household's independence.

Airlie engaged Peat Marwick McLintock (already the Queen's auditors) to undertake the review. Their aim was to re-establish the royal household as a strong bastion for an independent constitutional monarchy. In 1986 they came up with a 1,500-page report containing 185 recommendations for change. The Queen accepted most of them, and over the next three years 160 were implemented. They modernized the household, setting up a proper personnel department, defining the role of the Lord Chamberlain, sorting out offices and introducing budgeting systems. The restructuring did not make Airlie or the consultant Michael Peat very popular in the Palace. 'It was a time to go around with your collar turned up,' Airlie said later, but he was determined. 'We want to be masters of our own destiny,' he said.

The successful reforms enabled the Palace to persuade the Treasury that the household should be given more independence. In 1990 Airlie argued the case with Mrs Thatcher. She asked tough questions but then agreed to allow the household to take control of the Civil List from the Treasury. In July that year the government announced this fundamental change, and an increase in the Civil List of 50 per cent to £7.9 million a year for the next 10 years (assuming a 7.5 per cent rate of inflation) to start from 1 January 1991. The royal household also regained responsibility for the management of royal property from the Department of the Environment in April 1991. The budget for this had been £21 million under the government, but the Palace managed to get the costs down to £17 million.

Meanwhile, Thatcher had now won three elections and served 11 years as Prime Minister. She had achieved a great deal and appeared to have reversed the long-term decline of Britain. But she was becoming increasingly estranged from her own party, particularly over such divisive issues as the poll tax – an attempt to impose a head tax on every registered elector. In November 1990 her rivals in the Conservative Party forced a leadership election. In the first ballot, Thatcher narrowly failed to win the majority required to remain as leader. The contest would have to go to a second ballot.

Wednesday, 21 November 1990 was a night of high political and constitutional drama in the House of Commons. MPs were rushing hither and thither; cabals were forming in corners, whips were hunting votes, lobbyists were pushing and pundits were pontificating. Numbers were counted, loyalties were whispered and switched. There was only one thing everybody wanted to know: what would Mrs Thatcher do next? At one stage a new rumour took off. 'She is going to fight! She'll pull the temple down! She'll go to the Palace!'

Having failed to win re-election as party leader on the first ballot, rather than face defeat on the second, Thatcher was said to be thinking of recommending to the Queen the dissolution of Parliament. She would force an election on her ungrateful Conservative colleagues. According to Charles Powell, she never actually considered using this 'constitutional sledgehammer' as Robert Rhodes James, historian and then MP for Cambridge, called it. She said later that she did briefly consider another sledgehammer – staying on as Prime Minister – 'because you don't have to be a party leader in order to be PM'. She had in mind her hero, Winston Churchill, who became Prime Minister in 1940 while Neville Chamberlain was still leader of the Conservative Party.

What might the Queen have done if Thatcher had gone to the Palace with this proposal? Because Britain has no written constitution, there is no rule book. The Queen would have relied on her advisers and on precedent.

She would have had the right to try to dissuade Thatcher. That is one of her so-called 'prerogative powers'.

If Thatcher had indeed requested the largest 'sledgehammer', a dissolution, the Queen could have reminded her that no prime minister had the right to 'demand' this. The monarch's refusal is a check on what has been called 'the irresponsible exercise' of a prime minister's right to request it. The Queen could have asked Thatcher, 'Is a dissolution the collective advice of the Cabinet?' Thatcher could not have answered, 'Yes.' The Queen might then have asked her to consult her colleagues again, and Thatcher would have been obliged to do so.

The rumours and suppositions illustrate an important factor. The conventional wisdom is that under our constitution the Queen has no power. That is not quite correct. As Robert Rhodes James has pointed out, 'Those who had casually written off the political role of the sovereign as something dead and buried a century ago were utterly wrong.' This sovereign has influence that can be deployed as power. It is based on the fact that she has reigned since 1952 and conducted herself so discreetly. Her unique experience and long reign give British politics a dimension they would not otherwise have. And that night in November 1990 showed there was something very important beyond the hubbub and cliques of Westminster: the monarch.

The worst fears of Tory backbenchers were not realized. Thatcher gave way. She remembers her last audience with the Queen fondly. 'She's a very understanding person, and I think, shall we say, that she understood…the rightness of the decision I was taking.' However, for Thatcher, 'It was very sad to know that was the last time I'd go to the Palace as Prime Minister after eleven-and-a-half years.' A few weeks later, Mrs Thatcher met one of the Queen's ladies-in-waiting and said to her, 'Please tell Her Majesty how much I am going to miss her and our private talks and how wonderful she was to me when I came to say goodbye.'

What the Queen really thought of Mrs Thatcher remains cloaked in the discretion of the Palace. She once asked Lord Carrington, 'Do you think Mrs Thatcher will ever change?' to which he replied, 'Oh no, Ma'am. She would not be Mrs Thatcher if she did.'

If the Queen had disapproved of Mrs Thatcher, she did not show it. After Thatcher's forced retirement, the Queen immediately gave her the Order of Merit and then the Garter, the two highest honours in her personal gift. In 1995 she attended the former prime minister's seventieth birthday party at Claridges, where she sat next to John Profumo, who had won widespread admiration by spending the years since his disgrace in 1963 working quietly and diligently for the poor and homeless. She was seen to enjoy herself enormously.

six

The Royal Paper Chase

The media has never been a lapdog to the royal family. In 1830 *The Times* wrote a stinging obituary of King George IV, saying, 'There never was an individual less regretted by his fellow creatures than this deceased King. What eye has wept for him? What heart had heard one sob of unmercenary sorrow? ... If George IV ever had a friend – a devoted friend in any rank of life – we protest that the name of him or her never reached us.' Queen Victoria was much criticized in the middle, reclusive years of her reign, and George V was unpopular during World War I because of his German family connections, which prompted him to change the royal family's name from Battenburg to Windsor. Deference and journalism have never been bedfellows, but that knowledge was no preparation for what was to hit the present Queen and her family during the course of her reign. One of the features of the time has been the growth of media power.

From the moment she acceded in the Kenyan fig tree, the Queen and her family became public property. Her cousin, Pamela Mountbatten, remembers her looking out of the window of the plane as they circled over London airport the next day. 'One thought, "Oh my God...it's the end of everything, it's the end of their private life. For the rest of her life it's going to be public commitment."'

At her coronation 16 months later, on 2 June 1953, the Queen made a series of sacred promises. Over and over, ever since, she has stressed her overriding duty to the nation. Her immediate family could no longer be her only priority – though she considers the family to be a vital structure which she has often praised in her broadcasts.

The Queen was now head not only of her own immediate household but of the extended royal family proper. She had to take the lead in the family's delicate

◁ Princess Anne, Prince Charles, Prince Edward and Prince Andrew, pictured with the Queen and Prince Philip at Balmoral in 1972, twenty years after the Queen came to the throne.

relations with her uncle, the Duke of Windsor. Her father had a difficult relationship with his brother, especially after King George refused to make Mrs Simpson 'Her Royal Highness' on her marriage. The Queen Mother saw the abdication as the principal cause of her husband's early death.

The Duke was invited to his brother's funeral, but without his wife; he had tea with the Queen, Prince Philip and the Queen Mother. When Queen Mary died in March 1953, he came, alone again, to her funeral but he was not invited to the dinner at Windsor Castle after the funeral service. Both the Queen and her Archbishop of Canterbury, Dr Fisher, agreed that he should not be invited to the coronation. Churchill was of the same mind. When the Duke questioned him, the Prime Minister replied that it would be 'quite inappropriate for a king who had abdicated to be present as an official guest at the coronation of one of his successors'. The rift endured.

For the Queen to come to the throne so young was unexpected and unwelcome, but she had a clear purpose and role. Prince Philip had to create both for himself. As Pamela Mountbatten remembers, 'He saw his real role in life as supporting the Queen. He loved her dearly and wanted to do everything he could to help her, not to get in her way, to support her and to help her behind the scenes.' But it was not always easy to know how, and Pamela Mountbatten said that there were times when Prince Philip 'obviously did feel that he was totally unnecessary and neglected'. He was a capable young man, doing well in his naval career, and almost certainly would have made Admiral. Now he found himself confined to Buckingham Palace, restrained by courtiers and suffocated by the structures of the Court, in which a male consort had no real part to play.

He tried to bring 'a breath of fresh air' into the Palace by encouraging efficiency and championing modernization. This caused a certain amount of friction amongst the old guard at the Palace, who did not particularly like being told what to do by this young, foreign upstart. And there were constant pinpricks to his pride. The historian Kenneth Rose has recorded one. The sovereign is colonel in chief of all five regiments of Foot Guards. Before her accession, Princess Elizabeth was colonel of the Grenadiers and, on becoming colonel in chief, she proposed to make her husband colonel. However, senior officers of the regiment chose an older soldier. In the following year, Prince Philip became colonel of the Welsh Guards instead. 'What is unique about us?' he asked an officer at dinner one night. 'I will tell you,' came the answer. 'It is the only regiment in which the colonel is legally married to the colonel in chief.' Later, he did become colonel of the Grenadiers.

A century before, Prince Albert had taken on the role of Private Secretary to Queen Victoria, dealing with her ministers and drafting her letters. That option was neither available nor attractive to Philip. Instead, he began to create a life for himself that involved many professions and many skills. He has become an expert in education, health, sport and conservation. He was a champion of the natural world long before 'the environment' became a fashionable cause. He has also been involved in science and technology, and has headed various organizations in these areas – for example, becoming Patron of the Industrial Society. He has been made Chancellor of Edinburgh, Salford and Cambridge universities, as well as the University of Wales. He has always taken a keen interest in young people and in sport, and is President of the National Playing Fields Association and Patron of the Outward Bound Trust.

His most far-reaching achievement has probably been the Duke of Edinburgh's Award Scheme. The idea came from his old Gordonstoun headmaster, Dr Kurt Hahn, who, in 1934, had founded the Moray Badge, which gave young people a sense of achievement through meeting various challenges. The Duke's project was launched in 1956. At the time it was privately derided by some politicians, but the scheme, which helps young people meet adventurous challenges, gain a sense of personal achievement and develop as citizens, has become a great success. Today over 100 countries participate in the scheme, and in total some four million young people have benefited from the awards.

Prince Philip was never an easy man. He was intelligent but impatient, warm but critical. His sports were polo, shooting, sailing and, later, carriage-driving, and he competed fiercely in all of them. Self-confident, perhaps excessively so, he expects the same certainties in others, particularly his children. He does not suffer fools at all, let alone gladly. 'I am not a graduate of any university,' he once told a group of rectors and vice-chancellors. 'I am not a humanist or a scientist,

The love between Princess Margaret (far right) and Group Captain Peter Townsend (top centre) was doomed by disapproval of his divorce.

and oddly enough I don't regret it. I owe my allegiance to another of the world's few really great fraternities, the fraternity of the sea. At sea you will find all the conflicts that man has had to contend with now and in the past: the fear of the unknown, the power which is greater than man and his machines, the necessity to reconcile human frailties to scientific gadgets.'

After the accession, the other two out of 'the four us' – Princess Margaret and Queen Elizabeth the Queen Mother – moved out of Buckingham Palace and into Clarence House. The Queen was concerned not to upset or upstage her indomitable mother, and, 50 years later, many aspects of Palace life remain unchanged 'because the Queen Mother likes it so'.

The story of Princess Margaret's life after the coronation was not a happy one; it was also a warning of some of the dilemmas the head of the royal family was to face later in her reign. After her father's death, the grieving Margaret had turned to the King's equerry, Group Captain Peter Townsend, for support and found love. Peter Townsend was divorced, and in those days even the innocent party to a divorce was cold-shouldered. When the Queen Mother and Margaret moved into Clarence House, he became Comptroller of the Household. In the summer before the coronation he declared his love to the Princess. Tommy Lascelles, then the Queen's Private Secretary, told him, 'You must be either mad or bad or both.' The Queen tried to be sensitive and sympathetic, while also mindful of her position as Supreme Governor of the Church of England. She was careful not to make a judgement on the relationship. She asked them to wait a year before going public, until the coronation was well past.

On the day of the coronation Margaret was seen removing a speck of fluff from Townsend's lapel. The very next day the New York press ran the story. Over a week later the British tabloid the *Sunday People* reported that foreign newspapers were saying that Princess Margaret 'is in love with a divorced man and that she wishes to marry him'. The story sparked the first royal poll carried in a newspaper: the *Daily Mirror* asked readers if they thought that the couple should be allowed to marry. The vast majority of the respondents were in favour.

According to the Royal Marriages Act of 1772, the sovereign and Parliament must give permission for any member of the family in the line of succession to marry. At the age of 25 they can marry without consent, but they will forfeit their royal rights and monies. Margaret was still only 22. Lascelles and Churchill, spurred on by his wife, were very much against the marriage, and that became the view of the Court and Cabinet. At the end of June, when Princess Margaret was on a visit to Rhodesia with her mother, Townsend was abruptly posted to the British Embassy in Brussels as an air attaché. He wrote to her daily. Later, as Margaret's twenty-fifth birthday on 21 August 1955 approached, the press piled on the pressure. 'Come on Margaret! Please make up your mind!' demanded the *Daily Mirror*. She was besieged by hundreds of journalists and photographers at Balmoral, and for weeks there was a torrent of newspaper speculation.

In these early years of the Queen's reign, the young royal family was fiercely protected from the press. The Queen had inherited her father's Press Secretary, the formidable Commander Richard Colville. A naval man, he had had no previous experience of the press. He told a Canadian journalist, 'I am not what you North Americans would call a public relations man,' and said, 'My job is for the most part to keep stories about the Queen out of the press.' He argued that the Queen's family was entitled to as much privacy as any other. But the Press

Council, the new industry watchdog that was supposed to invigilate the conduct of newspapers, replied that the private lives of public people had always been the subject of natural curiosity, and that 'everything therefore that touches the Crown is of public interest and concern'.

If the press received no guidance from Commander Colville, neither did Peter Townsend, who later wrote, 'Since I was so closely bound up in Princess Margaret's future, it might have been better if Richard Colville, instead of leaving me to cope alone, had co-operated with me. But not once, during the whole affair, right up to the bitter end, did he contact me or attempt to evolve a joint front with me towards the press.'

The Queen apparently felt her sister must be free to make her own decision. One friend spoke of the Queen's difficult situation: 'She wanted Princess Margaret to be happy, very much. But then all her advisers told her that marriage just was not possible. And if Princess Margaret had married Peter Townsend, then she would have to lead a very, very different life.' Many of those opposed to the marriage argued that the Queen was the Head of the Church of England, and the Church did not recognize divorce. (Ironically, the new Prime Minister, Anthony Eden, was the only British prime minister ever to have been divorced.) *The Times*, then far more influential than now, published an editorial on 26 October 1955, stating that what was at stake was the image of a model family that the royal family was entrusted to display throughout the Commonwealth. Margaret's proposed union was something 'which vast numbers of her sister's people, all sincerely anxious for her lifelong happiness, cannot in conscience regard as a marriage'. She could not marry Townsend and remain officially a member of the royal family.

Margaret and Townsend decided, after reading this editorial, that they could not go ahead. On 31 October she issued a statement: 'I would like it to be known that I have decided not to marry Group Captain Peter Townsend. I have been aware that, subject to my renouncing my rights of succession, it might have been possible for me to contract a civil marriage. But, mindful of the Church's teaching that Christian marriage is indissoluble, and conscious of my duty to the Commonwealth, I have resolved to put these considerations before others.' Privately, she was devastated. Much later she said to the Queen's biographer,

Elizabeth Longford, that if she had been properly informed of the situation in 1953, she and Townsend would have broken off their relationship there and then.

The Queen did all she could to guard a private life for herself and her family. There were the long summer holidays together at Balmoral. At other times, they would have a weekend away visiting family friends, such as Lord Brabourne and his wife Patricia Mountbatten, or Lord and Lady Rupert Nevill in Sussex. Friends remember them as a normal, affectionate young family. Another family friend, Lady Kennard, talks of seeing them on holiday at Balmoral, where Philip used to play with the children during the day and read to them at night. In those early years, the Queen joked around a lot. Whoopee cushions were a favourite. Games such as sardines, blind man's buff, or stone, a version of tag in the dark, were played at home and in the country houses of friends.

The Queen sometimes went with close friends to the theatre or cinema. This could cause a stir. Patricia Mountbatten remembers going to the cinema with the Queen, Prince Philip and her husband to find that they were sitting in front of a row of Russian trade union delegates, who could not believe their eyes when the lights went up. They would never have seen Bulganin, let alone Stalin, in the next row of the stalls. On one occasion when Pamela Mountbatten organized an outing for her father, Lord Mountbatten, and the Queen, they were shown to their seats by the manager of the theatre, only to find other people sitting in them. The occupants were somewhat unwilling to move until they realized who was standing in the aisle.

In 1956–7 Prince Philip took a long voyage in *Britannia*, touring Ceylon, Malaya, New Guinea, Australia, New Zealand, Antarctica, the Falklands and other South Atlantic islands, and the Gambia. Back home, questions were asked about the length of time he was spending away. There were rumours, reported in newspapers, that the Queen's marriage was in trouble. When Eileen Parker, wife of Mike Parker, the Prince's Private Secretary, began divorce proceedings on the grounds of his adultery, speculation about Philip – always thought to be a bit of a ladies' man – increased. The Queen and Prince Philip both valued Parker and asked him to stay but, with the press pursuing him, he felt he could no longer perform his job properly, and he resigned from the Prince's service. He was much missed.

The American press was full of stories of Philip's involvement with an unnamed 'other woman' and the strain on the royal marriage. Commander Colville issued a statement saying, 'It is quite untrue that there is any rift between the Queen and the Duke.' This gave the British newspapers, irritated that an American paper had got a statement from the man who never gave them the time of day, the perfect opportunity to run the story. The rumours quietened down when the Queen flew out to Lisbon to join her husband, and the couple appeared happy and relaxed in each other's company. In fact the marriage prospered. A friend recalls that one evening 'the Queen was looking ravishing after a formal dinner. Prince Philip smiled at her and said, "You look good enough to eat." She blushed with pleasure.'

The press homed in on Prince Charles when he became the first future monarch to attend school. His first day at Cheam Preparatory School in 1957 was greeted with a flurry of press attention. Commander Colville called newspaper editors to the Palace and laid down an ultimatum – if they didn't leave Charles alone, he would have to leave school and be educated at home. The press backed off.

The question of the family name arose again because Lord Mountbatten and Prince Philip were still keen to have the Queen's heirs called Mountbatten. Harold Macmillan told of how, at the end of 1959, he arrived at Sandringham, to be welcomed by the Duke of Gloucester, the Queen's uncle. The Duke, according to Macmillan, was flustered and said, 'Thank Heavens you've come, Prime Minister. The Queen's in a terrible state: there's a fellow called Jones in the billiard room who wants to marry her sister, and Prince Philip's in the library wanting to change the family name to Mountbatten.'

Macmillan proposed that the royal family in future be called Mountbatten-Windsor and predicted Mountbatten would soon disappear from use, which it did. As for the 'fellow called Jones' in the billiard room, that was the society photographer Antony Armstrong-Jones, who had indeed proposed to Princess Margaret. After the Townsend debacle, the promise of happiness for the Queen's sister was widely welcomed. The Queen created Armstrong-Jones the

Princess Margaret and Antony Armstong-Jones, Earl of Snowdon, whom she married in 1960.

Earl of Snowdon, and the wedding was televised live on the BBC, gaining a world-wide audience of 300 million people. The publicity did not end with the wedding; their friends were chic and talkative, and from now on society columns were littered with references to the glittering couple.

The 1960s saw the arrival of one of the first paparazzi photographers with an intrusive telephoto lens – Ray Bellisario. Editors who used to publish Bellisario's material called him 'The Peeping Tom the Royals Dread'. Compared to the paparazzi photographs of today, his material seems quite mild. He sent the Queen a specially bound copy of his book *To Tread on Royal Toes,* which contained 120 unauthorized photographs. It was returned with a note: 'The Private Secretary to the Queen is commanded to acknowledge Mr Ray Bellisario's letter of 20th November and the copy of the book which accompanied it. Her Majesty does not wish to accept the book and it is therefore being returned herewith.'

As the family grew in the 1960s, with the arrival of Prince Andrew and Prince Edward, it became ever more appetizing to the media. The Palace began to learn that they could no longer rely on any tradition of deferential restraint. In June

In recent decades the Queen and other members of the royal family have had to become inured to the packs of photographers who pursue them.

1963 the 14-year-old Charles, in his second year at Gordonstoun School, took a sailing trip to Stornoway, on the Isle of Lewis. Charles and four other boys were allowed to go ashore for dinner and then to see a film. They were accompanied by the Prince's private detective, Donald Green. By the time the group got to the Crown Hotel, a small crowd was dogging them. Prince Charles recalled to his biographer, Jonathan Dimbleby, 'desperately trying to look for somewhere else to go' and heading into the bar. When he found himself there, 'I thought, "My God! What do I do?" I looked round and everyone was looking at me. And I thought, "I must have a drink — that's what you are supposed to do in a bar."' As a confused Charles went up to the bar and ordered a cherry brandy, the only drink he could remember in his panic, a journalist walked in and made the incident front page news.

Dimbleby records how Charles and his detective were bundled into a Land Rover and driven back to Gordonstoun. The Prince lay on the floor of the car covered by sacks to protect him from the photographers. He got a firm dressing down from his headmaster. But it was the removal of his private detective, whom Charles thought was 'the most wonderful, loyal, splendid man', that hurt the most. He later reflected, 'I thought it was the end of my world.' It was certainly a sour taste of what was to come.

In 1964 the Queen complained to the Press Council about pictures taken in Sunninghill Park, near Windsor, where she and Margaret liked to picnic. The Palace considered the pictures, published in the *Sunday Express*, offensive as they were 'taken surreptitiously and when the subjects were obviously unaware of the presence of photographers'. The privacy of the royal family was again invaded in October 1968 when the *Daily Express* published an old family photograph of the Queen in bed with her baby Edward. Buckingham Palace protested, and other papers expressed outrage. But the *Daily Express* took out a full-page advertisement in *The Times* to answer its critics. In the end no one at the Palace made a complaint to the Press Council, and complaints made by five members of the public were dismissed. Prince Philip loathed the papers, none more than those owned by Lord Beaverbrook. The *Daily Express*, he said, was 'a bloody awful newspaper'. Later he came to blame 'Murdoch and Murdochism' for the most intrusive assaults on the family.

In 1966, the BBC's flagship current affairs programme *Panorama* made a well-considered but quite tough film on the job of the Queen and its importance to Britain. It raised many questions about the style of the monarchy. The Palace was under increasing pressure to make itself more accessible. In 1968, Commander Colville retired and was replaced by William Heseltine, a young and open-minded Australian, who had already worked for several years at the Palace. Heseltine reflects, 'I was quite a different kind of person from Richard Colville and I think perhaps I had a slightly different attitude towards the job. I did tend to think that the strategy of keeping the private and public lives far apart had perhaps gone a little too far.' He thought that complete lack of access to the private life of the royals had made them 'rather one-dimensional figures' in the public's eyes. Another courtier says, 'By this time, the Queen was seen as living in another world, remote, stuffy and rich.'

Lord Brabourne, Patricia Mountbatten's husband, a film-maker and close friend of the royal couple, had noticed that because there were 'a lot of articles saying no one knew the Queen or the family' some newspapers had started inventing stories. Over lunch one day he suggested to Prince Philip that they make a TV documentary about the royal family. Philip said that he thought it was 'an interesting idea' and he would take it to the Queen. Heseltine remembers that the Palace was then being inundated with requests for press access to Prince Charles, who was being invested as Prince of Wales the next year. This film seemed to provide a solution. Richard Cawston, head of the documentary film department at the BBC, was chosen to make the film.

Before the filming began the Queen got keenly involved. She instructed Cawston to be placed next to her when the family was dining informally so that they could discuss the scenes. According to Douglas Keay, author of *Royal Pursuit*, she even went out of her way to arrange one particular sequence in which President Nixon met Prince Charles and Princess Anne, as 'we must have something special for our film'. The electrician on the film, Dave Gorringe, says the Queen was very interested in the process. 'She would suggest cuts at some times and could talk about angles of filming,' and told the crew about what to expect on certain occasions such as big banquets or investitures.

There were inevitably moments of awkwardness before the family got used to the cameras and the big fluffy microphones. Brabourne remembers, the Queen 'got a real shock' at a reception at the Commonwealth Heads of Government Meeting in London. She was talking to various dignitaries when 'suddenly she looked down and there was a microphone'. The Queen carried on faultlessly, even though normally such conversations are private, but she did say to Brabourne later, 'You know you never warned me. I didn't expect to see that fluffy thing.'

When Prince Philip saw the first version of the programme, his only complaint concerned a scene in which the four-year-old Prince Edward cried after being hit in the face by a string snapping on Charles's cello. Heseltine argued successfully that it was a very natural moment, obviously not staged, and should be included.

The film, entitled *Royal Family*, was shown on the BBC on 21 June 1969 and 23 million people watched it. The film was repeated on ITV eight days later, and

Prince Charles and Prince Edward in a scene from the television film *Royal Family*, which showed the Queen's private life for the first time.

altogether the BBC estimated that 68 per cent of the British public watched on both channels. It was sold to 140 countries. For viewers this was the first opportunity to see the annual pattern of the sovereign's life, to hear her voice and see her in informal settings. Today much of the footage seems stilted, and only young Edward seems blissfully unaware of the camera. The most memorable scene was the picnic at Balmoral, with Philip and Anne presiding over the barbecue while Charles tossed the salad with his mother. There was a charming glance of affection between mother and son. Heseltine remembers after the press viewing one journalist came up to him and said, 'Well, I expect all that food from the barbecue was thrown away.' Heseltine replied, 'If you think that, you don't really know very much about the Queen.'

Arguably, *Royal Family* was the first step on a slippery slope that led to the media rampage of the 1980s and 1990s. Cawston remembered David Attenborough, the anthropologist and then Controller of BBC2, warning him: 'You are killing the monarchy, you know, with this film you're making. The whole institution depends on mystique and the tribal chief in his hut. If any member of the tribe ever sees inside the hut, then the whole system of tribal chiefdom is damaged and the tribe eventually disintegrates.'

The theatre critic Milton Shulman was clear, as were many, that it marked a new age in the representation of the royal family. 'What has actually happened,' he explained, 'is that an old image has been replaced by a fresh one. The emphasis on authority and remoteness which was the essence of the previous image has, ever since George VI, been giving way to a friendlier image of homeliness, industry and relaxation.' He had a note of warning: 'Judging from Cawston's film, it is fortunate that at this moment of time we have a royal family that fits in so splendidly with a public relations man's dream. Yet is it, in the long run, wise for the Queen's advisers to set as a precedent this right of the TV camera to act as

Prince Charles and Princess Anne were introduced to President Nixon during the filming of *Royal Family*.

an image-making apparatus for the monarchy? Every institution that has so far attempted to use TV to popularize or aggrandize itself has been diminished and trivialized by it.'

Martin Charteris told me many years later that there was no alternative to being more open at the end of the 1960s. 'And, after all, the open door did not harm the Queen herself. She just carried on doing her job with her usual caution and dignity.' But the film did stimulate an appetite. Opening up may have been inevitable, but the family had breached the walls from the inside, and from now on many journalists, editors and proprietors would consider it a legitimate target.

In May 1972 the Queen went to Paris and visited the Duke of Windsor, who was dying of cancer. There had been sporadic contacts since the mid-1960s. In 1965 the Duke went to a London clinic for an eye operation and the Queen saw him briefly. She then invited the Duke and Duchess to the unveiling of a plaque to Queen Mary at Marlborough House in 1967. Since then, younger members of the royal family, as well as Lord Mountbatten and the Queen herself, had visited the Windsors in France. When he died, 10 days after the Queen's visit, his body was flown back to England and buried at the family burial ground in Frogmore, Old Windsor.

In 1973, Princess Anne became the first of the Queen's children to marry; she chose Captain Mark Phillips, a good-looking army officer who shared her love of horses and show-jumping. They had a son, Peter, born in 1977, and a daughter, Zara, in 1981.

Princess Margaret — the victim of hostile attitudes towards divorce in the 1950s — became the first in the Queen's immediate family to divorce in the 1970s. The media exploited Margaret's marital problems with Lord Snowdon. Indeed, through its wall-to-wall coverage the press was becoming a serial spoiler as well as a sententious chronicler. In 1976 the *News of the World* published pictures of Princess Margaret holidaying on the Caribbean island of Mustique with a much younger man, Roddy Llewellyn. This was said to have led to Lord Snowdon moving out of their marital home, and the couple's announcement that they were to separate.

Newspapers wrote pious 'Who is to blame?' editorials, and some even hypocritically asked themselves and their readers whether the media had played a role in the stress and ultimate failure of the marriage. However, the papers could not have asked for more from Roddy Llewellyn. Eighteen years younger than Princess Margaret, he revelled in the media attention, and took £6,000 from the *Daily Express* for photographs of him and his friends. He even attempted to launch a pop music career.

The Palace was also dealing with stories about the Queen's cousin, Prince Michael of Kent. He declared that he intended to marry an Austrian divorcee, Marie Christine von Reibnitz, whose father was reported (correctly) to have been an SS officer. She was a rather loud woman who became known in the press as 'Princess Pushy'. All of this was a nightmare for the Palace press office. One of its problems in the new age of intrusion was its strict rule, broken only in exceptional circumstances, never to deny a story printed about the royal family.

The family received a terrible blow at the end of the 1970s when Lord Mountbatten was murdered by the IRA. On 27 August 1979 a bomb blew up his fishing boat near his holiday home in the Republic of Ireland. He was on board the boat with his eldest daughter Patricia, her husband Lord Brabourne, their twin boys, Brabourne's elderly mother and a local Irish boy. Mountbatten, one of the twins, the Dowager Lady Brabourne and the Irish boy died; the rest were badly injured.

Mountbatten had been central to the royal family. He had played a role in the Queen's marriage to his nephew Philip. A man of great vanity who often infuriated politicians, he was devoted to the monarchy. He and the Queen were fond of each other, although she knew he was indiscreet. Perhaps even more importantly, he had become a vital friend and confidant of Prince Charles. 'Life will never be the same now that he has gone,' Prince Charles wrote in his diary the day he heard the news.

Another cause of change during the 1980s was the rise in the number of mass-market publications and the ever fiercer fight for readers. In the past, editors had

Lord Mountbatten was a close confidant of Prince Charles; his murder by the IRA in 1979 was a terrible blow to the Prince.

exercised restraint, fearing that intrusions into the private lives of the royal family would upset readers and damage sales. When this was no longer seen to be the case, the royal family became the top prize in the circulation wars. Every tabloid paper had a royal correspondent, and the broadsheets gradually followed suit. Journalists and editors began to treat the royal family as a rich source of scandal and innuendo, confident in the knowledge that the Palace would not deny any story, let alone sue.

The beginning of the 1980s' tabloid wars coincided with a feast of 'royal romances'. Newspapers had been speculating for years on Prince Charles's choice of bride. Many young women had been subjected to press attention, if not harassment, if they were seen as possible future princesses. Some were scared off. None had the impact of Lady Diana Spencer.

As soon as it became known that she was an object of the Prince's attention, the aristocratic 19-year-old nursery school teacher was under siege. Initially, she seemed to handle the pressure well – coquettishly but firmly. However, when in November 1980 the *Sunday Mirror* ran a story alleging a night-time rendezvous between Lady Diana and Prince Charles on board the Royal Train in Wiltshire, no one was amused. Certainly neither mother. The Palace demanded a retraction. Lady Diana's mother, Mrs Shand Kydd, wrote to *The Times* to complain.

Lady Diana was also upset when a journalist claimed that she had told him, 'I'd like to marry soon'. She tearfully denied ever saying any such thing. David

Chipp, head of the Press Association, checked the reporter's notebook, which apparently corroborated the story, and was annoyed when the Queen's Private Secretary, Sir Philip Moore, rebuked him nonetheless.

In January 1981 the press laid siege to Sandringham when Lady Diana was staying there. The *Observer* ran a story entitled 'Royal Family's Fury at the Siege of Sandringham', and quoted a spokesman as saying, 'The Queen is finding this intrusion quite intolerable and is more than a little angry about the behaviour.' A *Sun* reporter claimed that her car had been struck by royal shotgun pellets.

Gone were the days when the papers folded at the merest hint of offending the Queen. Indeed, the *Sun*, owned by Rupert Murdoch, claimed itself to be offended by the Palace: 'The monarch is now held in higher esteem than ever – thanks partly to the major reporting role played by the popular press. But the unfortunate – and we believe, temporary – breakdown in good relations has hardly been helped by Mr Michael Shea (the Queen's Press Secretary). His "contribution" has been to leak to the posh papers the information that the Queen is being hounded... The press is not there to persecute her. Its natural and legitimate goal is to photograph the lady who may be the next Queen of England.' The pressures on Charles, from the expectant world and from those around him, became immense.

For all her remarkable qualities, Diana was not the perfect English rose that the press liked to present. There were those who thought that she and Charles were so unlike each other that marriage would be a disaster. Diana's father, Earl Spencer, is said to have told the Queen that his daughter would be unable to cope. Charles's friends Nicholas Soames and Penny Romsey were against the marriage. So was Diana's grandmother, Ruth Fermoy, a lady-in-waiting to the Queen Mother, though she did not say so at the time.

Apparently the Queen kept her own counsel, as she often does. She has never been an activist chief executive of the family 'firm'. After his father urged him to make up his mind in order to protect Diana's reputation, Prince Charles took the plunge. He proposed to Diana on 6 February 1981. 'I do very much want to do the right thing for this country and for my family,' he said, 'but I'm terrified sometimes of making a promise and then living to regret it.'

On 24 February the engagement was officially announced, to the joy of the press and much of the world. A few days later Diana moved into rooms at Buckingham Palace, where she later claimed she felt trapped and friendless. There are reports that she first became bulimic at this time. Prince Charles was perplexed by her 'other side' but ascribed it to the immense pressures upon her.

Michael Shea tried to introduce Diana formally to the media. She saw a news programme being made at ITN, went to newspaper offices and even manned the Buckingham Palace press office phones incognito. But the attention began to become unbearable. Shea said, 'I can remember driving across Vauxhall Bridge with her before she was married, when she suddenly said, "Oh my God, look at that." And on the far side of Vauxhall Bridge there was a huge poster of her, which said "Diana – the true story". She started crying and said, "I don't think I can take this." The cracks were there.'

The media and public saw none of these difficulties and greeted the marriage of the Prince and Princess of Wales on 29 July 1981 with delight. It was a difficult time in Britain: the Thatcher government had embarked on its painful economic restructuring, unemployment was soaring and race riots tore through the hearts of several cities in the summer of 1981. Around the world over 700 million people are said to have watched the wedding on television. As Lady Diana arrived in her carriage at St Paul's, a BBC commentator said in hushed tones, 'There's a bride any man would be happy to see coming down the aisle…there is an air of mystery about her as she takes this longest and happiest walk she will ever take.' The Archbishop of Canterbury, Dr Robert Runcie, spoke of it as the 'stuff that fairy-tales are made of'. *The Times* declared, 'The English throne is now identified with exemplary family life.' And the *Telegraph* believed the royal family to be 'a symbol of hope and goodness in public life'.

Aware of press hunger for photographs on the return from their honeymoon, Prince Charles invited photographers to Balmoral in September 1981 so that they could take pictures and leave. But, when the couple announced in November that they were expecting their first child, press obsession grew again. Michael Shea invited editors of the national newspapers and BBC and ITV news to Buckingham Palace to tell them of the Queen's concern that the press attention

The Times declared of the wedding between Prince Charles and Lady Diana Spencer in 1981: 'The English throne is now identified with exemplary family life.'

was having on Diana. The only editor to decline the invitation was the *Sun*'s Kelvin McKenzie, who claimed that he had a prior engagement with his proprietor, Rupert Murdoch. The meeting at which Shea asked the reporters to treat Diana with more kindness and to leave her some privacy was followed by drinks with the Queen, when she made her attitude towards the tabloids very clear. The *News of the World* editor asked, 'Why can't the Princess send a servant to buy her fruit gums?' if she didn't want to be photographed. The Queen replied, 'That's the most pompous thing I have ever heard,' much to the delight of other editors.

The next day the columnist Peter McKay wrote in the *Express*, 'Now that the Queen has made known her feelings it would be a foolhardy editor indeed who ignored her request.' It soon became clear that there were such editors around. The *Sun* and the *Daily Star* sent their most aggressive royal reporters and photographers to hunt down the couple on holiday in the Bahamas. They were not disappointed. After struggling through shrublands and high temperatures with long-lens cameras, both came back with pictures of a pregnant Princess Diana in a red bikini. Michael Shea quickly made the Queen's displeasure known, describing the pictures as being 'in the worst possible taste'. The Press Council condemned both papers after an inquiry. There was a motion against them in Parliament and other tabloids criticized them. It made no difference.

Some respite for the couple came when the press decided to focus on Prince Andrew, who was dating the model and sometime soft-porn star Koo Stark. A photographer found himself on the same plane as the Prince, who was going on holiday to Mustique. The pack set off in full cry.

But no one could rival Diana's position as queen of the tabloids. Sales of a magazine would increase by 20 per cent if Diana appeared on the cover. The writer Auberon Waugh said, 'If she'd been a model, and had been paid for every picture that's appeared of her, she'd have been able to buy Buckingham Palace.' The Princess was the best ever meal ticket for both journalists and their employers.

During recent decades the tabloids have developed an obsession with sex and with the cult of celebrity. Royals now vied with stars and starlets in the media's insatiable search for sensation. Not only real people but fictional characters from soap operas such as *Dynasty*, *EastEnders* and *Coronation Street* became front page news.

At first the marriage between Prince Charles and Princess Diana appeared to be gloriously happy.

Actors and actresses were deliberately confused with their screen personas. It became harder and harder for readers to discern what was fact and what was falsehood or fantasy. In celebrity journalism such a detail hardly mattered. The royals had become 'Palace Dallas'. The journalist Nicholas Wapshott warned in an article in *The Times*, 'There is a delicate balance beyond which the Queen, once revered, becomes a celebrity like any other, open to abuse and ridicule like the rest. Familiarity can lead to more than just contempt.'

It is said that for a period in the early 1980s the press office at Buckingham Palace kept a file of untrue stories, but it had to be abandoned as 'it took up too much time.' And too much space, no doubt. Kelvin MacKenzie, editor of the *Sun*, was quoted as saying to his staff, 'Give me a…Monday splash on the royals… Don't worry if it's not true – so long as there's not too much fuss about it afterwards.' Donald Trelford, editor of the *Observer,* wrote, 'The royal soap opera has now reached such a pitch of public interest that the boundary between fact and fiction has been lost sight of…it is not just that some papers don't check their facts or accept denials: they don't care if the stories are true or not.'

The Queen managed to remain out of the front line of the confrontation. Her biographer Ben Pimlott wrote, 'Her exclusion was not a matter of loyalty. It was more that, unlike some of her relatives, the monarch did not talk to the press, did not row in public, and even in private kept a closely guarded tongue.' The Queen's silence, her refusal (like her mother) ever to give interviews or talk to the press, is probably one of the principal explanations for her comparative invulnerability. She remains mysterious, an enigma.

The distinction between royalty and celebrity became increasingly blurred. Prince Andrew went on the *Wogan* chat show, and the Prince and Princess of Wales were interviewed by Sir Alastair Burnet in 1985 when they took the opportunity to complain about media intrusion.

In the summer of 1985 Prince Andrew began to court a jolly, red-haired young woman called Sarah Ferguson. At first the press hailed her as a breath of fresh air in the family. On 23 July 1986 they were married as Duke and Duchess of York, with an estimated 500 million people watching on television around the world.

In 1987 Prince Edward proposed that members of the royal family should appear in a royal version of *It's a Knock-Out*, a TV game show with madcap physical tasks. Edward had to get permission from his mother, who was nervous about the idea, as was nearly every senior member of the royal household. Prince Charles and Princess Anne were opposed, but Edward was persistent and his mother was indulgent. He finally won agreement that the show could go ahead so long as the royal participants – Edward himself, the Duke and Duchess of York and, despite her better judgement, Princess Anne – only captained the celebrity teams and did not take part in the games. It still made for agonizing viewing as the Duchess of York yelled from the sidelines, and the celebrities made mock gestures of deference towards the royals. Prince Edward made matters worse by expressing his annoyance at the reporters' scepticism. 'Thanks for being so bloody enthusiastic,' he said. 'One of these days you lot are going to have to learn some manners.'

The show raised a million pounds for charity, but all agreed the Queen should have stopped her family from taking part. Martin Charteris said, 'The trouble with behaving like everyone else is that you get treated like everyone else. The Queen has succeeded because she has never done that.'

By the end of the decade the Palace began to respond, and there were a few

The Princess of Wales and the Duchess of York became the favourite prey of photographers during the 1980s.

victories. In October 1988 the *Sun* had to pay the Queen £100,000 as compensation for publishing a private picture of herself, the Queen Mother, the Duchess of York and Princess Beatrice. Princess Margaret's son, Viscount Linley, successfully sued the tabloid newspaper *Today* after it wrongly reported that he was ejected from a London pub for throwing beer. Koo Stark won £300,000 from another tabloid, the *People*, which claimed that she had continued her relationship with Prince Andrew after her marriage. In 1989, the editor of the *People*, Wendy Henry, was fired when her employer Robert Maxwell and the Palace objected to the publication of photographs of Prince William urinating on a school outing. And the Prince of Wales extracted an apology from the *Sun* in 1990. It had published a photo of him embracing Lady Romsey with the caption: Charles 'holds old flame Lady Penny Romsey in a lingering, warm embrace at a hideaway villa in Majorca'. It did not mention that her husband was only yards away, nor that the photograph was taken at the moment they had told Prince Charles that their four-year-old daughter, Leonora, had been diagnosed with terminal cancer. Two days later the *Sun* apologized.

Meanwhile, the press regularly had one target in their sights. Prince Philip was continually mocked by journalists who hung on his every gaffe – what he has called 'dontopedalogy', a tendency to put his foot in his mouth. The *Independent* wrote, 'The Duke of Edinburgh is an equal opportunities gaffemaker, not discriminating between countries and social strata when it comes to saying offensive or embarrassing things.' For example, on the royal tour to China in 1986 he remarked to a British student that he would get 'slitty eyes' if he stayed in China for too long. The British press was full of the 'Chinese fury at royal clanger'. However, when the Foreign Secretary, Geoffrey Howe, apologized to Chinese officials, they said there was no problem for they knew Prince Philip to be a sincere man. This was not the view the British press wanted to promote. Apparently, the Duke remarked recently to a friend, 'I have become a caricature. I've just got to live with it.'

At the end of the decade, the Royal Soap Opera took a turn for the worse. Princess Anne had been the first of the Queen's children to marry and she became the first to divorce. The *Sun* tried to claim the moral high ground when it announced, on its front page in 1989, that although it had received love letters written to Princess Anne, it had given them unpublished to Scotland Yard. A few days later a rival paper printed the name of the writer, Timothy Laurence, the Queen's naval equerry.

The content of the love letters led to a series of articles on the unhappy state of Princess Anne's marriage. She and her husband decided to separate and then divorce. In 1992, Tim Laurence became her second husband. Princess Anne had always had a tense relationship with the press. She once told reporters to 'naff off', and on another occasion she told a dinner given by the Associated Press, the American news agency, that journalists who peddled 'unadulterated trivia' should be given the Norman treatment: 'I am tempted to suggest the re-introduction of the Norman law where a slanderer not only had to pay damages but was also liable to stand in the marketplace of the nearest town, hold his nose between two fingers and confess himself to be a liar.'

Princess Anne has earned respect through her dedicated work for the Save the Children Fund.

But the Princess's public standing has since risen as a result of her dedicated charity work, and because she is totally discreet. Since 1970 she has been President of the Save the Children Fund and has worked tirelessly with the charity to alleviate the suffering of children in developing countries. She is also patron or president of nearly 100 other organizations, and undertakes about 500 public engagements every year. She is widely seen as hardworking and sensible, if occasionally abrupt. In June 1987, the Queen awarded her the title Princess Royal as a special honour in recognition of her work.

While Princess Anne's ratings went up, the Duchess of York's went down. She was an early target of the press's campaign to raise moral standards. It has to be said that she was often her own worst enemy. The £3.5 million Dallas-style ranch she and her husband built in Sunninghill Estate, Surrey, was seen as too ostentatious. She was also accused of cashing in on her royal status with her children's book *Budgie the Helicopter,* and she was criticized for charging *Hello* magazine £50,000 to photograph her family. More dangerously, her partying at a restaurant during the build-up to the Gulf War in 1991 sparked press complaint. *The Sunday Times* led the outcry by asking, 'Don't they know there's a war on?' and cited other examples of royal fun during times of crisis. In 1991 a *Sun* telephone poll asked 'Should Fergie leave the country forever?' Seventy-two per cent of callers thought she should.

In the 1990s the royal family lost the battle for privacy. There was no longer any accepted code of behaviour in Fleet Street to hold back stories. Worst of all, much of the most damaging material was shown to have a ring of truth. The last resort for the family in its fight for privacy was the Press Complaints Commission, the successor to the Press Council. In 1991, the Duke of York made a complaint to the PCC about a picture of his naked baby daughter, Princess Eugenie, published in the tabloid newspaper, the *People*. The PCC found in favour of the Duke, condemning the paper for its invasion of privacy and warning that this kind of behaviour could provoke government legislation. But the paper refused to back down. The editor Bill Hagerty and the proprietor Robert Maxwell struck back, first by asking their readers whether they thought the photograph was improper, and second by writing a letter to *The Times* criticizing the ruling and the threat of legislation.

But it was the Prince and Princess of Wales who excited most attention. By the second half of the 1980s their marriage had become more and more unhappy. The Queen and Prince Philip were aware of the difficulties but like many parents in such situations, it was unclear to them how they could best help. They had hoped that motherhood would bring Diana the happiness that had previously eluded her. It did not. The Princess continued to suffer from bulimia and sought refuge in some intense friendships – she became especially attached to one of her policemen, Barry Mannakee, who was tragically killed on a motorbike. She later fell in love with a Guards officer, James Hewitt. Meanwhile Charles turned for comfort to an old love. He and Camilla Shand had been close in the 1970s when he was in his early twenties, but she had married Andrew Parker Bowles, an officer in the Guards.

By now tabloid investigation and gossip was disclosing the unhappiness of the Prince and Princess and, perhaps, provoking it. There is a real question whether any marriage, let alone a troubled one, could survive the media pressures to which the royal marriages have been subjected in recent years. Press competition for exposure has been relentless. No other European royal family is at the mercy of such ruthless investigations. The King of Spain, for example, is rumoured to have a colourful private life but this is not reported, and the Spanish public adore him.

By the 1990s, it was not just the tabloids that delved into the royal marriages. *The Sunday Times* launched a campaign to persuade its readers there was a 'royal problem'. The paper warned that if the royal family carried on like this, a republic

The failure of the marriage of the Prince and Princess of Wales was a personal tragedy for them, as well as a tragedy for the monarchy.

was inevitable. The *Daily Telegraph* noted that the royal family was more criticized than at any other time in the century.

The hypocrisy that attended much of the criticism was breathtaking. Most moral and sexual taboos have disappeared since the Queen was crowned, yet newspapers sought to chain the royal family to standards that most of us would never expect to keep, while at the same time demanding that they lead normal lives in other respects. The press's commercial imperatives aside, perhaps the real source of the tension is that we still believe that one of the royal family's functions is, in writer Rebecca West's phrase, to hold up to the public 'a presentation of ourselves doing well'. When some of them do badly, we do not like what we see of ourselves.

The approach to the Queen's fortieth anniversary on the throne was sombre. There was uninformed talk in 1991 that she might use her Christmas broadcast to announce her abdication. This was nonsense: abdication is not a course she has ever considered. Instead she used the broadcast to emphasize once again her commitment to the nation: 'With your prayers and your help, and with the love and support of my family, I shall try to serve you in the years to come. I feel the same obligation to you that I felt in 1952.'

seven

Abroad and at Home

Since her accession, each year of the Queen's life has followed a meticulous routine. Her children were brought up around the calendar of the constitution. The Court moves between royal residences – Buckingham Palace, Sandringham, Balmoral, Holyroodhouse and Windsor Castle – according to an established seasonal pattern. The Queen spends the majority of each year in London, at Buckingham Palace, where she is involved in investitures, Privy Council meetings, and receiving ambassadors and foreign dignitaries. Throughout the year there are receptions, garden parties and visits to hospitals, schools, businesses, industrial plants and places of worship.

The Queen receives foreign heads of state to the UK, and goes abroad on state and Commonwealth visits. Wherever she goes, she is followed by her red boxes, crammed full of state business, which must be dealt with every day of the year, except Christmas and Easter. She has visited every Commonwealth country, except a new member, Cameroon. She was the first monarch to go to Russia and China. These visits are important. Even some of the host prime ministers have been taken aback by their success.

On the Queen's 1968 visit to Brazil, there was a minor crisis when a power cut occurred in the middle of a ceremony at the presidential palace. The whole place was thrown into darkness. 'There was the usual panic which takes place in high places when something like this happens,' says Lord Chalfont, then a Foreign Office minister. 'There were people rushing round with candles and torches and the whole thing looked as though it might descend into chaos. But the Queen, who is an enormous professional at this kind of thing, just carried on as though nothing had happened and this put all the other guests and the hosts at ease.'

◁ The Queen is at heart a countrywoman. Balmoral, her home in Scotland, offers her privacy in a place of great beauty. Riding has always given her a sense of independence.

Huge crowds attended her every stop. Sir William Heseltine, the Queen's Press Secretary, recalled, 'On the day we were in Brasilia the results of the American election were announced. Richard Nixon became President. But we had to read through about five or six pages of details of the Queen's visit in the local paper before we could discover who'd become President of the United States of America.'

Prime Minister Lee Kuan Yew was, he says, 'agreeably surprised' by the response to the Queen when she came to Singapore for the first time in 1972. He remembered, 'The people came out in droves to surround her car and wave. I had not expected that. I suppose there was a certain mystique about royalty. Her Private Secretary, Philip Moore, told me, "Don't push the crowds away, let them come. It's good for her."' Lee said, 'I glimpsed a certain satisfaction in her that she could arouse enthusiasm, in strange peoples, in strange places.'

Sir Sonny Ramphal, Foreign Minister of Guiana at that time, recalls how the young Michael Manley, Prime Minister of Jamaica and someone with 'anti-monarchical tendencies', agreed to host the 1975 Commonwealth Heads of Government Meeting in the Caribbean. Manley was nervous and asked, 'Look, is this going to be a problem, am I going to be in trouble, how are Jamaicans going to react?' Ramphal replied without hesitation, 'You have absolutely nothing to worry about. The Queen is going to be a star, and the visit is going to be marvellous.' He was right: 'It was a whopping success.'

Sometimes on her tours the crowds have been so large and enthusiastic that they have caused the Queen's party considerable concern. In 1976, she visited the United States to take part in the country's bicentennial celebrations. In Philadelphia, she began her speech with the words, 'I speak to you as the direct descendant of George III,' and then said that the Founding Fathers had taught Britain 'to know the right time and the manner of yielding what it is impossible to keep'. (That lesson had helped Britain transform the Empire into the Commonwealth.)

Michael Shea, who helped with the press on the tour, recalls, 'I can remember her coming out of a church on Wall Street. She was meant to do a walkabout down Wall Street, and security just fell apart: the crowds were pushing in so closely that we had to force a way through. There were plenty of police around but they were overwhelmed by the enthusiasm. There wasn't a hostile note anywhere; it was a jolly occasion, but very frightening because, of course, crowds can be frightening.'

The fear is often that those in control of the crowds panic and become rough. In states where the press is government-controlled and the head of state rarely, if ever, comes into contact with real people, the police have no idea how to cope. Sometimes the royal party has had to form a cordon around the Queen to protect her.

The Queen is always loath to cancel a planned tour. In 1979, before her trip to the Gulf, the Shah of Iran seemed to be about to fall from power. 'There was quite a lot of pressure from Prime Minister Jim Callaghan to cancel the Queen's visit to Iran,' said David Owen, the Foreign Secretary at the time. 'She did not want to do so; she wanted the Shah to do it, if he had to – and eventually he did. The Queen held out for that.'

In 1980, the Queen's tour of Morocco was a severe test of her diplomatic patience. The problem was the capricious nature of the monarch, King Hassan II. 'He makes the time. So it's no good asking what time he's going to arrive anywhere. He arrives at the King's time,' said Lord Chalfont. 'On that visit there was a certain amount of stress because the King kept the Queen waiting. And however important you may be, and the King of Morocco was a very important man, you don't keep the Queen of England waiting. This became a bit of a sensation in the press, and even in the royal party it was not regarded as being very polite.'

The visit did not get off to a good start. On the first evening, the Queen was left waiting in her car due to the late arrival of King Hassan at the banquet to be held in her honour. Matters got worse the following day when the King went to his air-conditioned trailer in the desert, leaving the Queen to wait a very long time while lunch was being prepared. His behaviour made the headlines in the British press. The King was furious.

Douglas Hurd, then a Foreign Office minister, recalls that the King sent his chamberlain to ask the Queen to postpone the dinner she was due to host on *Britannia* by one hour. 'I went to see the Queen and said, "What do we do now?" She replied, "Of course I can't change it. People have been invited for such and such an hour and there's no way of reaching them all and saying it's an hour later. But please tell the chamberlain that I will quite understand if His Majesty is delayed."'

The King arrived with some princes who had not been invited and in a great rage because his request had not been acted on. He could not be angry with the Queen, so he took it out on Hurd. 'I had an extraordinary evening. The King was sitting on the Queen's right and I was sitting on the King's right. With the Queen he conducted a fairly inane conversation about personalities – he was rather frightened of her I think. But with me, because he was in a furious temper, he was hissing in French… "I'm not being treated like a gentleman, it's all going wrong, that steel mission we were talking about on the train this morning, I'm not going to receive it, I don't have time, and what's more your ambassador has to leave Morocco tomorrow."

'I was quite inexperienced then and I didn't know what the hell to do,' said Hurd. At the end of the evening, while the Marines were beating the retreat, he

King Hassan frequently kept the Queen waiting during her state visit to Morocco in 1980.

President Ronald Reagan went riding with the Queen in Windsor Great Park in 1982. He found her a good horsewoman and 'charming, down to earth'.

asked Prince Philip's advice. The Prince knew the King. He said, 'Do absolutely nothing.' This proved good advice. 'The next day it was all smiles and presents of carpets and everything was fine, and the ambassador in question was knighted by the Queen on *Britannia*,' said Hurd.

During her trip to the United States in 1983, President and Mrs Reagan were very keen that the Queen visit their ranch in the hills above Santa Barbara in California. The weather was awful: many roads were flooded and the tracks up to the ranch were almost impassable. Charles Anson, who at the time was an official at the British Embassy in Washington, remembers, 'There were huge torrents running. The only way to get up was in four-wheel drive Cherokee vehicles, which the White House was reluctant to recommend to the Queen. But the Queen said, "If we can do it, let's go"... I suppose with the Queen's country upbringing it was not unusual... But it was something that struck the Americans: I think they called it plucky.' Nancy Reagan said, 'We were full of apologies to her about the rain and the fog but she kept saying, "No, no, this is an adventure!"' She greatly enjoyed lunch at the Reagans' ranch, saying later that politics were never discussed.

The storm meant that they were unable to travel in *Britannia* from Santa Barbara to San Francisco. President Reagan's aide Mike Deaver arranged for the best floors of the St Francis Hotel in San Francisco to be cleared for the royal party, and furnished with objects and pictures from the city's museums. They had unexpected time on their hands, so Deaver asked if the Queen would like to go to Trader Vic's restaurant. She and her party had a wonderful evening drinking rum punches and daiquiris. The Queen spent a good deal of time studying the menu and marvelling at the prices. She told Deaver it was the first time for 17 years that she had been to a restaurant.

Lord Chalfont says, 'She has a very real sense of the people and the traditions of the country she's visiting. She does her homework. Wherever she goes, whoever she meets, however large or small the country or the occasion, she prepares. She knows who she's going to see and she knows the background.' Geoffrey Howe, former Foreign Secretary, recounts that before her visit to China in 1986, she was told all about the Chinese leader, Deng Xiaoping – 'all the special sensitivities, his passion for smoking, his enthusiasm for bridge, his whole history'. During a lunch with Deng, the Queen noticed he was fretting uneasily. She leaned across to Howe and said, 'I think Mr Deng would be rather happier if he was told he was allowed to smoke.' Howe added, 'I've never seen a man light up more cheerfully. It was a very human touch and he appreciated it.'

The Chinese were eager to please. On the Great Wall the Queen and Prince Philip photographed each other – happy family snaps, thought Howe. He reflected on the 'theatre of monarchy'. 'We got tingles down our spine, on the deck of the royal yacht watching the Royal Marines beating the retreat in Shanghai. It's something that's never happened before and you feel a huge thrill and you can sense the people around you responding and feeling that it's part of something that they're never going to see again... I think that a monarchy enables you to stage a better piece of international theatre than other arrangements.'

During her historic visit to Russia in 1994, officials tried to separate the Queen from the people. When she went to Red Square, it was empty. 'The authorities played safe, they cleared the square, a huge great place – so the royal party wandered about rather unhappily with Yeltsin and no people,' said Douglas Hurd. It was disappointing. But, he added, 'The Russians realized their mistake because by the time we got to St Petersburg the mood had changed, the regulations had changed, the whole thing became more informal and more successful.'

Hurd commented that the Queen is practised at deflecting political questions. 'She will say, "That is very interesting, Mr President. I'm sure the Foreign Secretary would like to pursue this matter with you."' Occasionally she feels free to make pointed comments to foreign heads of state. Hurd remembers, 'When Yeltsin dined on *Britannia* in St Petersburg, he was banging on, as politicians do, about how he was sick of it all and he didn't think he'd stand again and so on. But it was fairly clear this was all shadow boxing and the Queen said to him, "I think, Mr President, you are going to stand again." This was a huge success. She ventured that far, but if he had gone on to make any more serious comments about his opponents or his policies, she would have certainly deflected it.'

On average the Queen hosts two or three state visits a year. The government suggests who should be invited, and with the Queen's agreement an unofficial sounding is made; if the response is favourable, an official invitation is issued. There is usually a 'waiting list' of about three years. Each visit takes about six months to plan. There is a basic routine. The visit starts on a Tuesday and ends on a Friday. Normally the visitors stay at Buckingham Palace, but sometimes they go to Windsor or Holyroodhouse. The head of state flies in on the Tuesday morning, and is met by a member of the royal family, who travels with them to London. There used to be a long carriage procession through London streets lined by guardsmen. The route is now much shorter (to avoid causing traffic jams and because there are fewer troops) but there is still considerable ceremony.

When the visiting head of state and his or her entourage arrive at Buckingham Palace there is a lunch for about 50 people. The afternoon is busy: engagements might include laying a wreath at the Tomb of the Unknown Warrior at Westminster Abbey, or a visit to another member of the royal family. In the evening, the Queen hosts a state banquet in their honour. The following day the visiting head of state is given a reception at St James's Palace with the High Commissioners and Ambassadors in London. They proceed to 10 Downing Street for talks with the Prime Minister and lunch. That afternoon they might have a press conference or meet other officials from their country or those in Britain. In the evening they attend a reception in the Old Library at the Guildhall and a banquet in the Great Hall, as a guest of the Lord Mayor of London.

On the third day the foreign head of state gets the opportunity to travel outside London and see something of the rest of Britain – perhaps a visit to a university or a factory. (The Palace would have found out in advance what might be of interest.) In the evening the visitor gives a return banquet in honour of the Queen and the Duke of Edinburgh. This is held either at the residence of their Ambassador or High Commissioner, or in a hotel.

On the Friday the head of state leaves Buckingham Palace at 10 a.m., after saying farewell to the Queen. Some choose to stay on in Britain for a few days, others fly off immediately. The Lord Chamberlain says goodbye on behalf of the Queen at the airport.

Not all visits are easy, and some are full of surprises. In 1973 President Mobutu Sese Seko of Zaire arrived for his state visit. Much to the surprise of the Palace officials who met him and his wife at Gatwick, Mrs Mobutu came off the plane clutching a dog, and a nurse followed behind clutching a child. Neither was expected. 'The sound of this dog barking in the Belgian suite at Buckingham Palace sent alarm bells ringing throughout the length and breadth of the Palace,' says William Heseltine. The Queen, concerned about rabies, immediately dispatched her precious corgis to Windsor, and sent Martin Charteris to tell Mobutu politely that the dog must be sent back to the quarantine kennels in Heathrow at once.

One of the most difficult occasions was the 1978 state visit of President Nicolae Ceausescu of Romania and his wife, Elena, arranged in the interests of Cold War diplomacy. It was an ordeal. The Queen had read all the Foreign Office telegrams about their abuses of power. 'They have blood on their hands,' she said to her staff.

Elena Ceausescu, who promoted herself as a scientist, got it into her head that she wanted to receive the very highest of British honours and awards. British officials thought that was going too far. The Ceausescus were also convinced that their rooms were bugged and brought their own team of security men who checked inside the lights and behind the gold panelling. They also had a problem with the British people's right to demonstrate. There was a palpable sense of relief in the Palace when the visit was over.

In the midst of her hectic schedule, the Queen has had to create the time to be a private person with her own pursuits. This can be difficult in a world where time always seems to be running out, where the goalposts for women as mothers, wives and professionals have changed dramatically and where the concept of privacy has been under constant, unrelenting and unforgiving assault.

When very young, Princess Elizabeth already had a particularly focused idea of what she enjoyed. Her governess, Marion Crawford, remembered the young Princess saying that when she grew up she would marry a farmer and have lots of 'horses, dogs and children'. Things did not turn out quite like that, but those close to her, such as her cousin Margaret Rhodes, still say that if she hadn't been

The Queen enjoys many country pursuits. Here she is pictured during gun dog trials at Balmoral in 1967.

Princesses Elizabeth and Margaret learned to ride as young children. Here they are pictured with their favourite groom, Owen, in 1933.

The Queen's skill as a horsewoman enabled her to control her mount, Burmese, when blank shots were fired during the 1981 Trooping the Colour.

Queen, 'she'd have been extremely happy breeding horses and dogs and leading the life of a country gentlewoman'.

For this reason the Queen particularly enjoys her private estates (run by Prince Philip) at Sandringham and Balmoral, where she can relax. Although she still has her red boxes, she is freer to decide what she wants to do.

Since she was a young child her abiding passion has been horses. Her grandfather, George V, used to take her around the stud at Sandringham. Margaret Rhodes says, 'I can remember many long hours playing at being a circus pony and that sort of thing when we were little.' Marion Crawford also recalled the little Elizabeth commanding an imaginary horse while sitting in bed. She was told, 'I mostly go once or twice round the park before I go to sleep, you know... It exercises my horses.'

Her grandfather gave her Peggy, her first pony, when she was four. Sylvia Stanier, who used to train the Queen for Trooping the Colour, says, 'She's a very fine horsewoman; she rides with a nice light rein. She's got great feeling for horses.' That was never more in evidence than on 13 June 1981, when a young man fired blank shots at her while she was riding Burmese at the Trooping. The horse was startled and shied, but the Queen remained in command and continued through the rest of the parade.

Another absorbing interest is racing (her mother's horses are steeplechasers; the Queen prefers the flat). She inherited this love from her great-grandfather, Edward VII. Lord Carnarvon, her close friend since the 1940s and her racing manager since 1970, remembered that her interest started when her father leased horses from the National Stud. 'Big Game and Sun Chariot were two frightfully good horses. They ran in the King's colours, and when he and Queen Elizabeth went down to Beckhampton to see the horses, they took Princess Elizabeth with them.'

The trainer Fred Darling notes that she has a fine eye for horseflesh. She has picked out classic winners just by watching them work on the downs. Once she was shown two yearlings, Doutelle and Agreement. The stable had got the horses mixed up. The Queen, who had only seen the pair as foals, was the first to notice and correct the mistake.

Her first racehorse, a filly called Astrakhan, came as a wedding present from the Aga Khan. Since then the Queen has bred many good horses and has won almost every classic. In 1953 she hoped to win the Derby with Aureole. The race was to be run the day after the coronation. It is said to have occasioned the following

The Queen used to love early morning gallops around the racecourse during Royal Ascot week. Press attention put a stop to it.

conversation between the Queen and a lady-in-waiting shortly before the ceremony in Westminster Abbey:

'You must be feeling nervous, Ma'am.'

'Of course I am, but I really do think Aureole will win.'

To her disappointment, the horse finished second, beaten by Pinza. After the race Norman Bertie, Pinza's trainer, was presented to the Queen. She congratulated him on winning the Derby. He replied, 'And may I congratulate Your Majesty on winning the world.' In 1954 Aureole won the King George VI and Queen Elizabeth Stakes at Ascot. Her great ambition is still to win the Derby.

Often the Queen's schedule prevents her from seeing her horses run, which is a pity for her and those who work with her. However, she can now watch important races on video. Until his death in September 2001, she talked to Lord Carnavon almost every day about which horses were racing where. He said, 'I always feel that racing has served her well – because she sometimes hears good news when a horse of hers has won. Normally most of the news she gets is bad. That someone has died or some accident has happened or something else unpleasant. I'm not talking about her family but about her responsibilities as monarch. At least when I ring up and say, "I've got some news for you, ma'am: such and such a filly won impressively," one feels one is giving her a bit of good news for once.'

Michael Oswald, her former stud manager, agrees. 'Racing is the one subject she can get deeply immersed in, if only for short periods, that is completely divorced from her everyday work. Even if the Queen is said to be on holiday, at Sandringham or Balmoral or somewhere, she's not really, because there's always a private secretary lurking around behind the corner, liable to come along with the boxes and more work. Now, if she can get involved in racing and breeding, if only for two or three hours, it's very good for her because she can switch right out of her everyday work which is always chasing her round.'

When she can, the Queen goes to the races; the Derby at Epsom and Royal Ascot are fixtures every year. Many of the photographs of her looking happiest have been taken at the races.

Racing is a passion that the Queen has inherited from her mother. It was a subject on which she consulted daily with her close friend and racing manager Lord Carnarvon (centre) until his death in 2001.

In 1974 she was overjoyed to see her horse Highclere win the highly coveted Prix de Diane at Chantilly in France. Earlier in the season she had watched the horse win the One Thousand Guineas at Newmarket and, as she left the enclosure, she was asked by the BBC's Peter O'Sullivan whether Highclere would run in the Oaks. Off the cuff she said, 'Well, I personally favour the Prix Diane. I don't think she'll come down the hill well at Epsom.'

Her racing manager Lord Carnarvon, her Private Secretary Martin Charteris and her stud manager Michael Oswald flew with the Queen to Chantilly. Joe Mercer was to ride. Carnarvon remembered the excitement of the French crowd. 'They went completely bananas, shouting "Vive la reine!"' when Highclere won.' Television film shows the Queen herself ecstatic in the box. As she went down to greet her horse and jockey in the winner's enclosure, her protection officer was swallowed up by the crowd. Oswald remembers seeing the Queen's pill-box hat bobbing up and down in the sea of people as he, Carnarvon and Charteris did all they could to push their way arm-in-arm to the enclosure.

On the plane home the Queen decided that the trainer and jockey should join them all for dinner at Windsor Castle. Joe Mercer remembers being in his plane half way over the Channel with Dick Hern, the Queen's trainer, and their wives when the message came through from the Queen's plane. At first they thought it was a joke. Then they worried that they were not wearing the right clothes. They were told to come as they were, and a very enjoyable and informal family dinner followed, with the Prix de Diane trophy in pride of place on the table. (At the end of the 1980s, after Hern had been paralysed in a hunting accident, his tenancy as the Queen's trainer was not renewed. His departure upset many in the racing world, who felt he had not been treated well enough. As in other parts of her life, the Queen's inability to reply to criticism counted against her.)

It is not just racing that the Queen enjoys. She breeds rather than buys horses. 'The real pleasure is in the stud farm, deciding which mare should go to which stallion, and thinking up names. She's very good at that,' said Carnarvon. 'Sometimes when the Queen is at Sandringham she sees foals born and then watches them throughout their lives, as yearlings, in training, being broken for racing and then, all too rarely I'm afraid, seeing them run.' The Queen has an encyclopedic knowledge of horses; she is said to know many bloodlines in great detail. She is also heavily involved in stable management.

Private holidays abroad have involved horses. She keeps mares in Bluegrass country in Kentucky, and has made private visits to check them. She has also made trips to Normandy to visit stud farms. According to Lord Carnarvon, who often accompanied her on these trips, on one occasion she was driving to see a French stud when she was asked, 'Why are they saying, "Vive la Duchesse"? Why not "Vive la Reine"?' She replied, 'Well, I suppose I am Duke of Normandy.'

The Queen has a natural affinity with animals and is fearless. Lord Carnarvon said, 'I've seen mares galloping around a field coming headlong towards her and the Queen never moves a muscle, whereas some of us are taking out our sticks, moving to defend ourselves.'

Along with horses there are the corgis. The Queen, like her mother, is famous for her devotion to the breed. Her first corgi, a male called Dookie, was brought into the household in 1933. A bitch, Jane, arrived to accompany Dookie, and a line was begun. Even on her honeymoon, the Queen's favourite corgi, Susan, went along. Living at Clarence House before her accession, she had time to take the corgis for a walk in St James's Park most mornings. At 4.30 p.m. each afternoon she would feed the corgis herself before having tea, a ritual that has continued throughout her reign.

The historian Kenneth Rose, with a wry eye for detail, has recorded that 'Susan begat Honey, who begat Bee, who begat Foxy, who begat Brush, who begat Geordie, who begat Smoky, who begat Spark, who begat Diamond. Going back nine generations in the Queen's family tree brings us to George I, who was born in 1660.'

Not everyone in the household is as fond of the corgis as the Queen. Her own footman also has to be a dog lover, capable of taking up to 11 corgis out for a walk at a time. The dogs do not like leaving their mistress and are often hard to control. Sylvia Stanier remembers that, when training with the Queen for Trooping the Colour, the dogs used to come too. 'The poor footmen would bring them out. They'd hear the Queen's voice and they'd rush up to the horse and follow her round. They wouldn't leave her and the footman had a terrible time trying to get them back in.'

She is good at dealing with corgi squabbles. Michael Oswald remembers, 'Once there was the most fearful dog fight. And she was far braver than anybody else. She plunged into the middle of this terrible mêlée and fished out the ringleaders.' If she ever gets bitten, she always says, 'It was entirely my fault.'

By accident one of her corgis once bred with Princess Margaret's dachshund. They called the product – Mr Pipkin – a 'dorgi', and the experiment seemed worth repeating. She has kept some of these dogs and given others to close friends and the wives of some of her senior staff if they are known to be dog lovers. Apart from corgis and dorgis, she is skilled at handling working labradors, spaniels and other sporting dogs. The main kennels are at Sandringham, and when the Queen is in residence she likes to help train the dogs. The kennels have produced some high-class performers, with Sandringham Sydney winning several field trials.

The former head-keeper Bill Meldrum remembers one occasion when he was on a shoot with the Queen, working their dogs. She asked Meldrum whether he could direct his dog to fetch a bird on a hill quite some distance away. Meldrum said he wouldn't be able to with the dog he had with him that day, but he thought the Queen might have better luck with her dog Sherry. Using whistle commands, the Queen sent Sherry several hundred yards away, and directed her to the exact spot where the bird had fallen. Behind her, the beaters and the guns stopped to watch. When Sherry picked up the bird and returned it to her mistress, the Queen was applauded by about 40 people. 'If I'd known they were watching, I wouldn't have attempted it,' she said.

When the Queen works her dogs out shooting, she is at times unrecognizable in her mackintosh and Wellingtons with a scarf wrapped around her head. On one occasion a keeper saw a small woman bending over a stream, holding on to a tree in order to hook a bird out of the water. He said, 'Look out little lady, you're going to fall in.' He was taken aback when he found out that the 'little lady' was in fact the Queen.

The Queen is blessed with an ability to switch easily between different subjects. Margaret Rhodes says, 'She is very lucky in having a sort of compartmentalized brain, which means that she can switch off from a particular worry, shut the door on it and carry on in a light-hearted and happy way. It's rather a fortunate thing to be able to do.'

Those who knew her well as a child remember her as a private, shy person, rather like her father. One close friend reflects, 'Over the years she has become much more relaxed and professional about meeting people, knowing what to say and enjoying it.' Those on the first Commonwealth tour in 1953–4 remember the strain of endless public appearances, especially the whistle stops where there were always small groups of people waiting at every crossroads to see her. Pamela Mountbatten says, 'I remember her saying, "Oh, Mummy would love this, she does it so well. I wish I could."' Others say that she is still slightly nervous before big functions, such as the State Opening of Parliament, but

A dynasty of dogs, particularly corgis, has followed the Queen throughout her reign.

once she gets going she is fine. Some have described her as 'slightly keyed up, not nervous' before she attends a large function, like an accomplished actress anticipating a performance. All remark on her professionalism when meeting people, and her ability to say the right thing to put people at their ease.

In *Britannia* life was easy. David Owen, who travelled on the royal yacht as Foreign Secretary, said that when the day's work was done there was a relaxed atmosphere and 'although you're an outsider and a politician, you are just treated like one of the family'. When all the guests had gone, 'you saw her at ease and, in many ways, a different person, witty and fun'. It was clear that 'this woman had much more depth, humour and warmth than she allows herself to present in her public persona'.

Just as she can never retire, she can never really be off duty either. But she tries to make a clear distinction between her public and private persona. Owen says, 'She definitely keeps the two in separate compartments; she thinks that's necessary to maintain the dignity of the office. She believes the monarch will not gain strength or stature by a sort of artificial folksiness, and I think she's right.'

As Queen she is aware of the importance of ceremony, but as a person she is rather humble. She has been known to say that events or people are 'far too grand for me'. She was genuinely touched by the public's warmth towards her during the Silver Jubilee celebrations. That sense of humility goes with a lack of vanity. She rarely looks at herself in the mirror. As a Princess and young Queen, she was dressed by Hardy Amies and Norman Hartnell. Both were fashionable at the time, but that was never the Queen's primary concern. She resisted the very short skirts of the 1960s, and the big shoulder pads of the 1980s. Her main priorities when choosing outfits for public occasions are that they are comfortable and that people can see her in them. Over-large hats are out of the question, as they are hard to be photographed in and are cumbersome in cars. She is not dogmatic about clothes but, if presented with something she is not keen on, is inclined to say, 'Do you really want me to look like that? Really and truly?' When the milliner Frederick Fox produced a tiny red straw hat for the Dubai Races, the Queen returned it to him, saying, 'You know it's too small… I think you've been looking at far too much *Edward and Mrs Simpson*, Mr Fox'.

All her friends speak of her sense of humour. She is an accomplished mimic, and her impression of Concorde landing is quite something. She is good at imitating politicians and modern music. She laughs easily. Once, when a young and eager private secretary told Prince Philip that he could not have another drink as they were about to disembark from *Britannia*, the Prince looked as though he would explode. The Queen thought it was hilarious.

Controlling her laughter is not always easy. On one occasion she arrived for the Maundy Service at Wells Cathedral a bit too early. When the bishops, who were not ready, saw the Queen they made a Monty Pythonesque run into position with their mitres bobbing up and down above the heads of the crowd. It took a while for the Queen and her entourage to regain their composure.

The Queen can also make jokes at her Prime Minister's expense. In 1977 Callaghan recommended to the Cabinet that they give the Queen a gift to mark the Jubilee. Shirley Williams suggested a saddle, Tony Benn a vase carved out of coal by a Polish miner. Callaghan decided to ask the Queen herself. She suggested a coffee pot. Roy Hattersley recalls, 'So we all turned up to present the coffee pot, and the Queen made a little speech in which she said, "I particularly want to thank the Prime Minister for his forbearance. When a similar occasion was held for Queen Victoria, the prime minister of the day, Lord Salisbury, thought the appropriate present was a portrait of himself. I'd like to thank the Prime Minister for not having the same idea on this occasion." Now, for the Queen to say this was just slightly daring, and we all laughed, and we all laughed genuinely.'

She has a gift for the crisp one-liner. When she was in *Britannia* with the Reagans in Santa Barbara, one of her staff remembers, 'People kept coming up to the President and saying things like, "Mr President, your thinking on Nicaragua this morning is as follows. And if you're asked about the Middle East, Mr President, this is what you should say. And, Mr President, if you're asked about the Federal Reserve Bank's policy, this is your thinking on that. And Mr President, here is your speech for this morning, and I'm sorry you haven't seen it until now but we've broken the big words up and we know you'll deliver it terribly effectively." Somebody near the Queen heard her say, "And they call me a constitutional monarch?"'

She can make her displeasure clear. One aide has commented, 'She could get really quite upset if she discovered that schoolchildren or elderly people had been out waiting in the rain for half an hour or an hour for her arrival.' She rarely complains directly if something goes wrong, but might say 'That was a very interesting experience', which means 'Don't do that again'. One of the Queen's old employees said he would never try to pull the wool over her eyes, and he knew that if he told her a lie, that would be it. Another courtier remarked, 'She is very friendly and easy to get on with. But there is, of course, a point beyond which you don't go, even in very familiar circumstances because the Queen remains the Queen.'

One person who has known her since before she came to the throne is King Constantine of Greece. He first met Princess Elizabeth when she and Prince Philip went on a tour of Greece after their marriage. Since the Greek monarchy was abolished, King Constantine has lived in exile in Britain and has become close to the Queen. He told me, 'She has the capacity of older European royals to look people in the eye and show them with one look that they have gone too far. My grandmother Olga froze out a group of Bolsheviks when they tried to seize her house during the Russian revolution. It's a great talent. The Queen has it too.'

Television provides the Queen with a window on the changing world – and also a way of following her racehorses.

In the early 1960s, when he was First Lord of the Admiralty, Lord Carrington says, 'I got a blistering rocket from her.' *Britannia* needed an extensive refit, which led at once to adverse press criticism about royal extravagance. 'I was called by Michael Adeane and summoned to the Palace. I knew by the tone of his voice that this was not going to be fun. I went in and was not asked to sit down. She asked me, "Who pays?" I said, "Oh, the Admiralty, of course, Ma'am." The Queen replied very coldly, "I see. You pay and I get the blame." I was shown the door.'

The Rev Anthony Harbottle was given 'the glance' in his first interview for the job of Chaplain to the Queen at the Royal Chapel of All Saints in Windsor Great Park. She asked him why he had taken up the ministry and he started to explain at length. 'I got rather enthusiastic, which was fairly natural I suppose, and suddenly this sort of iron curtain descended, and the Queen just looked at me completely expressionless. I had been told before that this does happen on occasion, and I realized that I was perhaps seeming to get a bit over the top. I immediately pointed out to her the relevance of what I was saying, and all was well.' He got the job and he never saw that look again. 'I'm glad I haven't, because it's pretty devastating, actually.'

She made it very clear to Geoffrey Rippon, then Environment Minister, how upset she was that in 1963 he had allowed the Hilton Hotel at the bottom of Park Lane to be built so high. Photographers could peer down into the gardens or private rooms of Buckingham Palace with their telephoto lens.

Roy Hattersley remembers going to Buckingham Palace at the time of the betrothal of Prince Charles and Lady Diana. The Queen remarked on the fact that the Spanish were objecting to *Britannia* calling at Gibraltar (which they laid claim to) on the couple's honeymoon. She said, 'I told them: it's my son and it's my yacht and it's my dockyard.'

Mary Francis, who moved from 10 Downing Street in the mid-1990s to become the first female Assistant Private Secretary to the Queen, saw similarities between the Queen and Mrs Thatcher. Their styles were completely different, she said, but with each of them, 'You saw everything judged against a very clear personal philosophy and reference points.'

Once Francis suggested the Queen make a joke about the satirical magazine

Private Eye. 'But she was very clear that nobody would believe that she read *Private Eye* and that such a joke would therefore be inappropriate for her.' She has a habit of simply not commenting on suggestions she dislikes. 'You just get silence – and you don't persevere,' said Francis.

Lord Airlie, the Lord Chamberlain, concurs. 'She leaves you in no doubt if she disagrees with a proposal,' he says. 'If I sent her a memorandum and did not get a reply in 24 hours, I could be pretty sure she was not comfortable with it.'

There are things over which the Queen has had no real control, such as the need to increase security during her reign. A good friend remembers that in the old days when the Queen came to stay she would just bring her own detective. The village policeman would come up at night, make himself a cup of tea and walk around the house. Since then, terrorism has made protection a very different operation; indeed, it is now one of the highest of royal costs. The Queen used to love to go Christmas shopping; department stores would open up an hour early so she could shop in peace. Now, because of both terrorism and the press, such trips have been stopped, and goods have to come to her.

Many of her associates have remarked on her nerve and her resilience. She is not easily scared. A close friend remembers going riding in Sandringham with the Queen on a particularly foggy day. As they got onto their horses, she remarked that she had just heard that the IRA had now got a new telescopic rifle that could see immaculately through fog. 'But it didn't stop her going riding.' And, as we have seen, when Burmese shied at the sound of blank shots during the 1981 Trooping of the Colour, she showed courage as well as skill by riding on regardless.

On 9 July 1982 the Queen was woken early in the morning by an unbalanced man in his thirties who had broken into the Palace and found his way to her bedroom. Michael Fagan said later that he wanted to talk to the Queen about his family problems, and had intended to slash his wrists in front of her. He had in his hand a broken glass ashtray. When she saw Fagan at the end of her bed with his head bowed, staring at his bloody hands, she said, 'I think you've come to the wrong room.' He did not leave. The Queen pressed her emergency buzzer twice and made two calls for the police but no one came. She then asked Fagan if he wanted a cigarette and when he said 'Yes', she used it as an excuse to leave the room. When everyone realized the enormous breach of security that had taken place, all hell broke loose, but the Queen as usual remained calm. She told her cousin Margaret Rhodes that it was not such an ordeal because she was used to meeting odd people in her line of work.

Like her father, the Queen finds it hard to express her emotions. Indeed, she controls them firmly. Her cousin Lord Harewood says that this is a family trait. He said of his parents: 'They found it as hard to talk in a serious yet personal vein to us as we did to them.' Even during the abdication crisis, 'the whole of my mother's family tended to bottle up their feelings very much. To the point of it being a fault…it was a tradition not to discuss anything awkward. But that went much wider than just the family. It was general in a way we find difficult to realize now.'

The Queen was brought up in the public eye in an age when almost everyone was taught that it was inappropriate to show deep emotions even in private, let alone in public. The war had this effect on many of her generation; every week more friends would be killed. People had to learn not to make a fuss. Displays of emotion were deemed unhelpful and out of place.

Her reserve is clear in public as well as in private. When, many years ago, she visited a school for the blind in Iran, the wife of the Shah, Farah Diba, went down on her knees to caress the children. The Queen did not. At the spectacular VE Day celebrations in Hyde Park in 1995, each head of state was led to the Globe of Peace by a child from his or her country. Almost all held the child's hand. Not the Queen.

But close friends insist that her reticence should not be mistaken for lack of emotion. They say that though she might not reach out and hug you, she will be thoughtful and concerned about your welfare, and she is a good listener. At times of emotional drama she seems to be cut off. She keeps even her husband and children at arm's length at such moments. It is almost as if she does not want to add to *their* grief. She will tell close friends (usually after the event) if she has been agonizing over something, but, like many of her generation, she finds it hard to confront her children's crises face to face.

If people do try to talk directly to her about painful topics, she might look embarrassed or change the subject or play with the dogs. This does not mean that she does not care, says one friend, but rather that she cares too much and is afraid of her own emotions. Her restraint, and Prince Philip's more argumentative and assertive personality, must have played a part in the emotional development of their children. It is undoubtedly true that her relations with Prince Charles are imperfect. According to a friend, there is underlying love but poor day-to-day co-operation. Their respective staffs are not always in unison either. (In recent years her caution about endorsing his relationship with Camilla Parker Bowles has added to the strain.) But surely the point is that all families have their own internal dynamics, which are usually impossible for spectators to understand. In the case of this family, however, commentators and critics are legion and observe no restraint.

She is concerned for, and considerate of, the people who work for her either in Buckingham Palace or on one of her estates. Kenneth Baker, whilst Chancellor of the Duchy of Lancaster (which embraces the Crown's estates), was impressed by the amount she knew about her tenant farmers and their families. One friend remembers her concern for a child whose parents worked on the Crown estates and who were going through marriage difficulties. She wanted to arrange the transport the child needed to see his mother. A woman working on the *Royal Family* film, who had a necklace of sentimental value stolen from her, was given another as a present from the Queen. She never makes such gestures ostentatiously.

The need to help those who are less fortunate or lonely is a theme of her Christmas broadcasts. She has, at times, adopted some touching imagery to describe how small practical gestures can bring pleasure to others. In 1988 she said, 'Recently, many of you will have set up and decorated a Christmas tree in your homes. Often these are put by a window and the bright and shining tree is there for every passer-by to see and share. I like to think that if someone who feels lonely and unloved should see such a tree, that person might feel "It was meant for me".'

It is worth repeating that at the core is her deep Christian faith. It is for this reason that her coronation meant so much for her. She not only was anointed –

The Queen's Christian belief is central to her life; her relationships with successive Archbishops of Canterbury, including the present Archbishop, George Carey, have been very important to her.

she *felt* anointed. One close friend said, 'I'm perfectly sure that for the Queen it was positively a sort of religious experience, which meant a huge amount to her.' She goes to church every Sunday without fail, and is in church quite frequently on more formal occasions. One of her friends has said, 'She is what you might call a traditional Christian.' Another says that the knowledge that some madman in a crowd could shoot her any day has always kept her close to God. 'She has her luggage packed and is ready to go.'

Her faith is unquestioning. Prince Philip, on the other hand, has a tendency to worry about issues. In the words of Bishop Michael Mann, the former Dean of Windsor, 'He has to know all the ins and outs of an issue. He's like a terrier pulling it to bits and then eventually he'll come up with what he believes. The Queen's belief is very much one of acceptance of the traditional faith she's been brought up in and known all her life. It is the absolute mainspring of her life. When she was consecrated she saw herself as set aside for a particular purpose. The whole

The fire at Windsor Castle in November 1992 destroyed state rooms, including the magnificent St George's Hall used for state banquets, before it was finally brought under control.

of her life has been dictated by a desire to do her duty and to fear God and to walk before Him humbly.'

Just as she recognizes that constitutional changes are beyond her remit, she accepts (perhaps with regret) the sometimes rather desperate changes the Church has wrought in its attempts to keep its congregations. For her the King James Authorized Version of the Bible and the Book of Common Prayer are the appropriate guides.

Her relationships with successive Archbishops of Canterbury are important to her. In recent years she enjoyed the company of Robert Runcie, who was urbane and intelligent and had served in the Scots Guards. She is said to have found his successor, George Carey, distant at first, but she has developed respect and affection for him, and asked him to remain as Archbishop until her Golden Jubilee.

She uses her Christmas broadcasts to express both Christian and non-denominational spiritual messages. These messages are not just to Britain but to the Commonwealth, where Christians are in a minority. She has often retold the Christmas story or some of the teachings of Jesus, and reflected on what it means to her people today. But she is well aware of the changes in religious practice. She said in her 1982 broadcast, 'At this time of the year, Christians celebrate the birth of their Saviour, but no longer in an exclusive way. We hope that our greetings at Christmas to all people of all religious conviction and good will be received with the same understanding that we try to show in receiving the greetings of other religious groups at their special seasons.' She realized that, 'To many of my people Christmas doesn't have the same religious significance, but friendship and good will are common to us all.' She warned against unthinking people who 'carelessly throw away ageless ideals', such as religion, morality in personal and public life, honesty and self-restraint.

The Queen's faith has supported her throughout her reign in a job that is very isolating. In 1947, during the royal trip to South Africa, her father turned to Field Marshal Smuts and said, 'There she goes, alone as usual, an extraordinary girl.' It is a theme that painters such as Annigoni have picked up on. In his lovely 1954 painting he portrayed her standing quite alone. He commented, 'I see her alone – alone against every tide.'

Never did her loneliness seem more apparent than on the day in November 1992 when her beloved Windsor Castle caught fire. Her coachman Stephen Matthews remembers the Queen standing alone in the courtyard in front of the burning Brunswick Tower. 'We could feel what she must be going through, and obviously wanted to comfort her, but no one had the courage to go and do it.' The coachman lamented, 'Although this woman's very powerful and much loved, no one can approach her in a personal way. And it must be a very lonely sort of position to be in.'

eight

The Young Prime Ministers

The year 1992 marked the Queen's fortieth anniversary on the throne, but there was hardly a mood of celebration. Her biographer Ben Pimlott noted, 'Newspaper profiles registered the date with sympathy more than congratulation.' The year began well, with an excellent BBC television documentary, *Elizabeth R*, made by Eddie Mirzoeff and Antony Jay with the Queen's full co-operation. It portrayed her work as a constitutional monarch and revealed much of her spirited and humorous personality. But the programme's beneficial effects were soon swamped by events, which tumbled over one another for several years to come.

In January, photographs were published of the Queen's daughter-in-law, the Duchess of York, on holiday with a man called Steve Wyatt. In March, the Palace announced that the Yorks would separate. The BBC Court correspondent was quoted as saying that 'the knives are out for Fergie' at the Palace. Charles Anson, the Queen's Press Secretary, denied saying any such thing, but he apologized to both the Queen and the Duchess.

A few months later came perhaps the most compromising pictures ever published of a British royal. They were of the Duchess of York having her toes attended to by her business adviser, John Bryan, and appeared in the *Daily Mirror* and *Paris Match*. The Palace objected, but even the monarchist *Daily Telegraph* felt that although the photographer 'behaved wrongly' and invaded her privacy, 'the Duchess had been behaving without dignity and sense'.

The Duchess of York's indiscretions were bad enough. More damaging were revelations about Charles and Diana's marriage. In June 1992 *The Sunday Times* began serializing a book by Andrew Morton, a member of the royal ratpack, called *Diana: Her True Story*. The book was full of allegations of neglect and adultery on the part

◁ The Queen inspecting fire damage to Windsor Castle in November 1992. The fire came to symbolize what she called her '*annus horribilis*'. She faced it with her customary stoicism.

of Prince Charles. No one at the Palace anticipated the impact it would have, nor did anyone have any idea how extensively Diana had co-operated with the author – she had denied doing any such thing. The book was unfair to Prince Charles, but it caused a new media frenzy, which became even fiercer when tapes of private telephone conversations between Diana and one of her admirers, and between Charles and Camilla Parker Bowles, were published.

The publication of the Morton book coincided with a state visit to France. The Queen fulfilled her programme so calmly, Charles Anson said, that 'One didn't really realize that there was anything else that she might have been concerned with.' The British press and a large part of the British public were obsessed with the revelations and scandals. On the Champs-Elysées the French were more concerned with watching the Queen.

Through this period of crisis the Queen came to count on Margaret Thatcher's successor, John Major. At 47, he was Britain's youngest Prime Minister since Lord Rosebery in 1894, and was just eight years old when the Queen came to the throne. Like so many others, his Christmas memories revolved around the Queen's broadcasts. He recalls, 'There was an absolute determination that it would not be missed, and I can never remember it being so.'

Like Thatcher, Major was a committed monarchist but he was more relaxed with the Queen than his predecessor had been. They formed a bond that was strengthened by the fact that both were under great pressure throughout his premiership. As Major wrote in his memoirs, 'My inheritance was unpromising.' Many Conservatives were bitter or guilty about the way Mrs Thatcher had been ousted, and the economy was in recession, with inflation and unemployment rising. Divisive rows over European integration dogged and dominated Major's government.

Major called an election for April 1992. During the campaign, the constitution became a serious issue dividing the parties. Labour was committed to radical constitutional change, which led Major to declare, 'The United Kingdom is in danger. Wake up, my fellow countrymen. Wake up before it is too late!'

Before the election many polls showed that the best Major could hope for was a hung Parliament. The Queen's prerogatives were again a live issue. There were constant discussions between Buckingham Palace and Number 10 about the circumstances in which the Prime Minister would go to the Palace to resign. His aide Sarah Hogg said, 'We had to revisit the doctrine, looking up all the informal papers, old letters to *The Times* and so on.' In the event, Major won the election.

In September 1992, Major faced the political horror of Black Wednesday, when speculators sold the pound short and Britain was forced out of the European Exchange Rate Mechanism. He called the Queen three times that day. 'She was very helpful and very sympathetic,' he said.

Like so many others, Major found the Queen's knowledge of the Commonwealth remarkable. He believed that affection for her was a potent force binding the organization together. She knew everyone, and everyone's father and everyone's foibles. At one Commonwealth meeting Major was having difficulty persuading a prime minister of something. When he told the Queen, she said, 'He's very fond of fishing, try that.'

They discussed almost everything at their weekly Tuesday meetings. 'What I found so valuable about the Tuesday meetings,' Major said, 'was that one can say absolutely anything to the Queen. Even thoughts you don't wish to share with your Cabinet at a particular time, you can say to the Queen, and I did… When you're prime minister, you're often boxed in, at least, that was my experience, and it is very useful to have that safety valve, someone you can say absolutely anything to.

'If the Queen is unhappy about something, she doesn't say, "Well, I really wish to warn you against doing that." But she talks about the subject. She says, "Well, how is that going to work? Is that going to cause a different problem?" It's really an intelligent discussion of the issue at hand. I don't think, on any occasion in my experience, she actually had to say, "I don't think you should do this" or "I do think you should do that".'

As she faced the humiliatingly public and long drawn-out breakdown of her two eldest sons' marriages, the Queen's Tuesday meetings with Major became almost mutual support sessions. Major knew that the scandals were devastating for her. He was dismayed by the mistakes of the younger royals and the press glee that he felt was bound to diminish respect for the monarchy. Nonetheless, he was kind to the Prince and Princess of Wales, meeting with both of them, and trying to be an honest broker. Each was grateful to him, but by autumn 1992 it had become clear that the marriage could not survive. Number 10 and Buckingham Palace discussed the constitutional implications at length.

In his memoirs, Major is so discreet about these unhappy events that he makes absolutely no reference to them. To have done so, he said, would have been 'utterly wrong… The discussions I had with the Queen were private and were meant to remain private… Those meetings were free, they were frank and I didn't think they were for general discussion subsequently.' To do so would 'destroy forever the bond of trust that exists between the Queen and her successive prime ministers'.

Then, on 20 November 1992, a dreary day, Windsor Castle caught fire. The Queen regards Windsor as home and loves it. The Lord Chamberlain, Lord Airlie, who watched the inferno with the Queen, says, 'Seeing the flames leaping into the

John Major with the Queen at Balmoral in 1991. Every September, the prime minister of the day spends a weekend with the Queen at her Scottish home.

sky was horrific and frightening. I felt very much for her; it was an appalling thing for her to watch. She was deeply upset but she was stoic. Somehow or other, she wasn't going to show how upset she was. She doesn't like to show her emotions. That's not the way she is.'

The Castle is state property and the fire damaged sections open to the public and some state rooms, not the private rooms. It used to be maintained by government ministries and, when the fire broke out, it was being rewired at government expense, therefore it was not unreasonable to assume that the government would pay for the restoration. The government announced that it would do so.

To Major's astonishment, a storm of protest, led by tabloids such as the *Daily Mail*, rejected the suggestion that taxpayers' money be spent on restoration. The message was that it was the Queen's problem. He was shocked. 'I have to admit, I completely misjudged the way people would react. I had thought that there would be the most tremendous outbreak of sympathy... I was astonished at the press campaign.' He considered it 'a very miserable and mealy mouthed response'. But it was a moment of grim truth for the Queen. The fact that a paper such as the *Daily Mail*, ostensibly conservative and monarchist, led such a bitter campaign and got government policy reversed, reflected some of the deep changes in the country.

The Palace decided to heed the outcry. The problem, Lord Airlie said later, was that the Queen could not afford to pay for the repairs herself. 'The cost turned out to be about £37 million. The Queen hasn't got that sort of money.' The press did not believe that – newspapers alleged her personal fortune to be between £100 million and several billions. Airlie gave a press conference at the time in which he said that even the estimate of £100 million was a 'gross exaggeration'.

The solution they found was to open Buckingham Palace to the public in the summer while the Queen was at Balmoral, and to charge an entrance fee to the precincts of Windsor Castle. The income generated by the Royal Collection Trust was also diverted to the restoration.

Four days after the fire, the Queen made an extraordinary speech at the Guildhall. She had flu and a temperature of 101, but insisted on keeping the date. Her voice hoarse, she said in a phrase that was to become so celebrated, that 1992 'is not a year on which I will look back with undiluted pleasure. In the words of one of my more sympathetic correspondents, it has turned out to be an *annus horribilis*.' (The correspondent in question was Sir Edward Ford, the former Assistant Private Secretary who had broken the news of her father's death to Winston Churchill in February 1952.)

The Queen was reflecting on the orgy of criticism in the press and on the changes in the country when she said, 'No institution – City, monarchy, whatever – should expect to be free from the scrutiny of those who give it their loyalty and support, not to mention those who don't... Forty years is a long time. I am glad to have had the chance to witness, and to take part in, many dramatic changes in life in this country.' Her pain, her grace under pressure and her humility were evident, and the audience gave her a standing ovation. Newspapers were less generous: the *Sun*'s headline was 'ONE'S BUM YEAR'.

A few days later, on 26 November, John Major announced that the Queen and Prince Charles had agreed to pay tax on their private incomes. This move had been under preparation long before the fire, but the timing made it look as if it was a direct response to newspaper attacks. In the same announcement Major also said that £900,000 worth of Civil List payments that went to five members of the royal family would end. Only the Queen, the Duke of Edinburgh and the Queen Mother would continue to receive direct Parliamentary annuities; from now on the Queen would reimburse the government for all the allowances given to her children under the Civil List.

Two weeks later, on 9 December, Major told the House of Commons that the Prince and Princess of Wales were to separate. He insisted, to the surprise of many members, that this would not affect Diana's right to become Queen. Major believed this was the correct position to take and said he was stating what was 'self-evidently the constitutional position'. Robin Butler, the Cabinet Secretary, recalls: 'We wanted to reassure people that even though there was a separation, this wouldn't prevent the Princess of Wales becoming Queen. With hindsight it was a mistake to have said that in the statement. But it was seen as softening the blow, showing that she was not being thrown into outer darkness.' And it was constitutionally correct.

Major ended the year by coming once more to the Queen's side. 'I believe [the monarchy] will weather the difficulties it has had in recent months and emerge strengthened,' he said. 'I detect no enthusiasm in this country for anything other than a continuation of the constitutional monarchy.'

In her 1992 Christmas broadcast, the Queen did not dwell on the horrors of her year; instead she said that talking to the humanitarian Leonard Cheshire, whom she admired and who was near death, 'did as much as anything to help me to put my other worries into perspective'. As she had throughout her reign, she pledged her 'commitment to your service in the coming year'.

The *Sun* decided to publish her Christmas message two days before Christmas. The Queen was distressed by this, but when her lawyers pursued the *Sun* for damages for breach of copyright, the paper remained unrepentant: 'We don't consider that we did anything wrong... We reckon that we already pay enough taxes to keep Her Majesty in the style to which she has become accustomed.' However, the paper then retreated, and wrote an open letter of apology to the Queen, agreeing to pay legal costs and give £200,000 to charity.

In September 1994 the Palace set up the Way Ahead Group. An in-house forum, it was chaired by the Queen and Prince Philip, and included their four children and senior courtiers. It was to meet twice a year to discuss reform and strategy for the monarchy, looking into all aspects of royal life from marriage to rules on succession. It was also designed to help the family to deal with problems that might arise before they became huge public issues.

That year the Queen was saddened by the government's announcement that the royal yacht *Britannia* was to be decommissioned in 1997. The entire family was distraught at the loss of the ship that had been their floating home and sanctuary for over 40 years. It had also been a superb platform on which to project Britain around the world, and it was said to have travelled more than one million miles on 968 official voyages. Many people regretted its loss, but no party championed the yacht; it was easily dismissed by the press as another example of royal extravagance that should be scrapped. Other seafaring European monarchs, including the Spanish, Danish and Norwegian, still have yachts.

Britannia was not the only loss the Queen felt deeply. In 1991, as a result of the end of the Cold War, the government published its Options for Change plans to cut the armed services. The proposed mergers of regiments deeply upset their members, from generals to private soldiers. Many wrote to complain to their colonel in chief, almost always a member of the royal family, and in many cases the Queen herself.

The armed forces have always been one of the most important pillars of the monarchy; similar notions of duty and honour have traditionally bound the two institutions. Different members of the royal family have formed close links with the regiments of which they are colonel in chief. The Queen, Prince Charles and other colonels in chief were saddened by the proposed changes.

Tom King, the Defence Secretary, went to Buckingham Palace to explain the proposals. With him went General Sir John Chapple, Chief of the General Staff. The meeting was not a happy one. Both men say that the Queen behaved absolutely properly, but she made her dismay at the scale of the cuts very clear, as had Prince Charles earlier to the Prime Minister. Tom King said afterwards, 'It was very hard for her. She was obviously very disappointed but behaved quite correctly at our meeting.' Chapple concluded: 'She showed a deep concern, based on her extensive knowledge, first in relation to the army's future, and of the men, their families and their regiments'. Her judgement proved better than that of the politicians. After a large contingent of British troops was sent to Bosnia on peace-keeping duties, Tom King's successor, Malcolm Rifkind, reversed some of the cuts and four historic regiments were saved.

Throughout this period, the Queen had to watch her eldest son being vilified, often outrageously, in the media for the failure of his marriage. She and Prince Philip were slow to understand the tragedy of Prince Charles's marriage, and she tried to be protective of Diana, though the Princess's unpredictability made that increasingly difficult. In 1994, on the occasion of the twenty-fifth anniversary of his investiture as Prince of Wales, Prince Charles did something his parents had never done – to pre-empt unofficial versions, he authorized a biography and a television film of his public and personal life, both by Jonathan Dimbleby. They were detailed and sympathetic. In the television interview Prince Charles admitted for the first time that he had not been loyal to Princess Diana after their marriage

The Queen feels a great affinity for the armed forces; the British military owe direct allegiance to the Queen rather than to the government.

had irretrievably broken down. This admission caused an extraordinary but predictable furore.

The Dimbleby book dealt with the Prince's entire life and praised his extensive charitable work, in particular for the Prince's Trust, which he had created to provide opportunities for the underprivileged. It also quoted friends of Charles who were privately critical of his parents for their lack of support through his marriage problems. The press, including *The Sunday Times* which serialized the book, seized on passages that seemed to show the Queen as distant and the Duke as overbearing, and the Prince as an unhappy child. The book itself also quoted Prince Charles as saying that his memories of childhood were very happy.

The book appeared as the Queen embarked on her successful tour of Russia. Even the media frenzy at home could not diminish the extraordinary impact of the historic visit in Russia, where Tsar Nicholas II, a cousin of the Queen's grandfather, George V, had been murdered by the Bolsheviks in 1918. 'People recognize the point of monarchy when the Queen goes abroad,' said Douglas Hurd, who accompanied her. 'The Queen evoked a sort of nostalgia, a sort of envy... It was remarkable in Russia, where they were groping for their own past.'

When the Queen went to South Africa the next year, Hurd felt that the visit was 'really rather a gamble' because 'it wasn't all that long since the British government [under Mrs Thatcher] had refused to apply sanctions against South Africa, and the leadership of the ANC, Mandela included, had been very critical of our stance'. So there was concern about 'how it would work out on the ground'. In the event, 'the reception in the townships was enthusiastic, overwhelming…great crowds of young black South Africans [were] chasing after the car, trying to keep up, waving and cheering.' The Queen strengthened a remarkable relationship with Nelson Mandela. They had met for the first time in Harare in 1991 and were described as 'getting on like a house on fire'. They had much in common: both had devoted their lives to duty.

The visits were covered in Britain, but the press was more interested in private unhappiness than in public triumph. With Princess Anne, Prince Andrew and Prince Charles now either remarried, divorced, or separated, there were gleeful accusations that the Queen had been a bad mother. Bishop Michael Mann, the former Dean of Windsor, considers that attack very unjust. 'I think she's been a very good mother. Like any parent she bleeds for her children in their difficulties or distress. To say it's her fault is very unfair. Other parents get sympathy in such circumstances, not criticism.'

In retaliation against her husband, the Princess of Wales gave a secretly filmed interview to the BBC's *Panorama* programme in November 1995. The BBC informed the Palace only shortly before they issued a press release, a week before the broadcast. The BBC's Director General, John Birt, had not told in advance his Chairman, Marmaduke Hussey, whose wife, Susan, was one of the Queen's longest-serving ladies-in-waiting and a friend of the Prince of Wales.

In the sensational interview, the Princess complained that her husband's relationship with Camilla Parker Bowles had made her marriage 'crowded', admitted her adultery with James Hewitt, made public her war with the Palace, talked of her husband's staff as 'the enemy' and speculated over whether Charles would ever be King. The interview divided the country in just the way that a monarchy is supposed not to do.

Diana called for 'clarity' and that was supplied by the Queen in an astonishing way. Setting aside her usual reticence in such matters, the Queen wrote to her son and daughter-in-law requesting that they divorce. As both head of the

The Queen's visit to South Africa in 1995 was a great success; she and Nelson Mandela established a warm rapport.

Church and as a mother, this must have been a very hard decision to make. The contrast with the predicament of Princess Margaret 40 years earlier, when she was compelled to forsake a man who had been divorced, was distressing. Complicated negotiations between lawyers about the settlement ensued. Finally, terms were agreed, and in August 1996 the Prince and Princess of Wales were divorced.

This wrenching, public unhappiness in the royal family coincided with the collapse of the Conservative Party. The politics of the early 1990s were dominated by allegations of misdoing by government ministers and by Conservative MPs. Disarray over Europe, dishonesty over arms sales to Iraq, sexual scandals, cash bribes in envelopes – all these dominated perceptions of Conservative rule by the mid-1990s.

Major called an election in May 1997 and lost in a landslide to Tony Blair's 'New Labour'. Blair's party had accepted many of the economic tenets of Thatcherism. This was inevitable. The 1990s had seen the birth of globalization, and economies were becoming more and more intertwined. No democratic government could control the means of supply within an old socialist framework. Douglas Hurd remarked that the Conservatives had lost the election but won the argument.

The morning after the election Major went, as prime ministers must, to tender his resignation to the Queen at Buckingham Palace. His wife, Norma, went with him. Major was moved; so, it is said, was the Queen. She talked to him at some length and put his defeat into the perspective of decades. When he left her office, Major, his wife, the Queen's Private Secretary, Robert Fellowes, and her lady-in-waiting Susan Hussey were all quite emotional.

At the Palace, they had to recover quickly. Twenty minutes later the victorious Tony Blair was due to arrive ; he would undoubtedly be feeling as high as Major was low. Some of those around the Queen fortified themselves for the mood change with stiff gins and tonic. One said afterwards, 'It seemed a microcosm of what the Queen has to do all the time. The Majors had become good friends and the Blairs were perhaps very nice but unknown. She has to dissociate from all emotion.'

Almost at once, Blair and his wife, Cherie, arrived at the Palace full of the thrill of victory. The courtiers congratulated him, and the Queen asked him to form a government. She then met with his wife and congratulated her as well.

Tony Blair was the Queen's first Prime Minister who had not been born when she came to the throne. He was the first to have no memories of the coronation whatsoever. A child of the 1960s, he called himself a modern man. His commitment to the monarchy was uncertain.

Then, in August 1997, the Princess of Wales died in Paris as her drunken driver sped to get away from the pursuing paparazzi. I briefly described in the Preface how the world reacted to this terrible event. With the passing of years, the response of the public and the media at the time seems all the more extraordinary.

The world and the royal family were rocked. The Princess's brother Charles was in South Africa, where he gave an immediate press conference in which he bitterly blamed the press for hounding her to death. The new government and the Palace were thrown together. For once in her life the Queen put her family before her country and stayed with her grandsons in the seclusion of Balmoral while, to everyone's astonishment, huge crowds of people, most of them young, gathered in London and elsewhere to grieve.

The royal family, and in particular the Queen, was attacked for not returning to London at once to grieve publicly. 'SHOW US YOU CARE' shouted the *Daily Express*; 'SPEAK TO US MA'AM' demanded the *Mirror*. One poll showed that seven out of 10 people thought that the Queen was 'out of touch', and the *Sun* went so far as to say, 'There has been no expression of sorrow from the Queen on behalf of the nation. Not one word has come from a royal lip, not one tear has been shed in public from a royal eye.'

Some believe that such media attacks on the Queen were deliberately made so as to deflect attention from Charles Spencer's serious charge that press harassment had led directly or indirectly to the Princess's death.

A vocal section of the public and the press demanded to know why Buckingham Palace was not flying a flag at half mast. Courtiers argued that there is never a flag over the Palace unless the Queen is in residence, when her Royal Standard flies. The Standard does not fly at half mast even when the monarch dies. Such arguments were not accepted; the empty flagpole was seen as emblematic of the Queen's lack of concern for the Princess and public emotions. By Thursday, precedent had been broken and the Union flag was flying at half mast.

The accusations made by the media ranged wide: it was alleged that the Queen did not want Prince Charles to take an RAF plane to escort Princess Diana's body from Paris, did not want her to lie at the Royal Chapel at St James's Palace, and did not want her to have a public funeral. Undoubtedly there were disagreements about how best to respond. There would be in any divorced family at such a terrible time, let alone in one under such public pressure. It is important to state that there is no evidence for such cruel accusations.

In fact many of the key decisions were made in the early hours of Sunday morning, immediately after the Princess's death, and long before the public reaction to the tragedy became evident. The Queen, the Prince of Wales and Robin Janvrin, the Queen's Deputy Private Secretary who was in London, debated through the small hours. They decided to wait until daylight to tell the boys. Their nanny crept into their room to take out the radios in case they turned them on and heard the news. When they awoke, their father told them what had happened, and asked them if they thought he should go to Paris to escort their mother's body home: they did. Diana's sisters, Sarah and Jane, decided to fly with him. The Spencers at first wanted the Princess to have a private family funeral but it soon became clear that that would be impossible.

Lord Airlie says that the arrangements for the Prince of Wales to fly to Paris were made within hours of the Princess's death, and that he began to plan the funeral that same day. Robin Butler, the Cabinet Secretary, confirms this. Furthermore, as soon as it was established that the law would allow the body to be taken to the Royal Chapel at St James's Palace, that is what the Queen agreed.

At Balmoral, Princess Diana's sons were in shock. It seemed to their family and to Court officials that they were unable to take in what had happened. On Thursday, the family decided to go once again to Crathie Church near Balmoral to attend a service for the Princess and to look at all the flowers that had been brought there. The Queen, the Prince of Wales and Bob Sloan, the Minister, devised a service that helped to comfort the bereaved.

The Palace informed the press that Princes William and Harry would be present. A swarm of photographers, television cameramen and journalists gathered outside the church to witness the family in sorrow. At one moment Prince Harry reached for his father's hand and suddenly scores of cameras clicked and whirred.

On Friday Prince Charles and his sons flew down to London; the Queen flew separately, as she is not allowed to travel in the same plane as her heir. That evening Prince Charles, William and Harry talked to mourners outside Kensington Palace. It is not hard to imagine what an ordeal this was for the boys. Their courage and dignity were remarkable. Then the Queen and Prince Philip arrived outside Buckingham Palace, stopped the car and talked to some of the thousands of mourners waiting there. This must have taken considerable nerve: no one knew what to expect. The Queen was treated with courtesy – people seemed relieved. She then walked into the Palace and at 6 p.m. made her extraordinary live broadcast to the nation. 'This week at Balmoral,' she said, 'we have all been trying to help William and Harry to comes to terms with the devastating loss that they and the rest of us have suffered. No one who knew Diana will ever forget her. Millions of others who never met her but felt they knew her will remember her. I for one believe there are lessons to be drawn from her life and the extraordinary and moving reaction to her death.

'I hope that tomorrow we can all, wherever we are, join in expressing our grief at Diana's loss and gratitude for her all too short life. It is a chance to show to the whole world the British nation united in grief and respect. May those who died rest in peace and may we, each and every one of us, thank God for someone who made many, many people happy.'

John Grigg, the early critic of her speaking style in 1957, said this speech was 'one of the very best of her reign. It absolutely put the crisis to bed and stabilized the situation.' That was perhaps achieved more easily than many expected because the anger was expressed by a vocal minority through the media, and did not represent the views of the mass of the population.

The funeral, arranged in only five days, was a mixture of ancient and modern. It was watched on television by an estimated 31 million people in Britain, and two-and-a-half billion people around the world. As the procession came by

Prince Philip, Prince Charles, Princes William and Harry, and Charles Spencer joined the funeral procession of Diana, Princess of Wales.

Buckingham Palace, the Queen led out the other members of the royal family to pay their respects. She bowed to the coffin as it passed – a moving moment.

In Westminster Abbey, Diana's brother, Earl Spencer, gave a tribute that seemed a rebuke of the Windsors. Speaking of Diana's sons, William and Harry, he pledged, 'We, your blood family, will do all we can to continue the imaginative way in which you were steering these two exceptional young men so that their souls are not simply immersed by duty and tradition but can sing openly as you planned.' He also attacked the press. The crowd outside watching the service on large screens applauded, and the sound rippled into the Abbey.

Diana's friend Elton John sang a specially adapted version of *Candle in the Wind* to her memory. One commentator remarked that it was as if Vera Lynn had sung at the funeral of King George VI. That would have been unthinkable in 1952.

Public reaction to the death of Princess Diana brought home to the nation, the people and the monarchy how much change had taken place in the country since the beginning of the Queen's reign, and how hard it was for the monarchy to keep abreast. It is still difficult to define just what the outpouring of emotion really meant. One argument, put forward by the constitutional historian Vernon Bogdanor, is that those people who mourned for Diana so openly, mourned the loss of a member of the royal family who had transformed their expectations of the monarchy.

Privately, Diana could be difficult to deal with. She exasperated not only members of her family but some officials of the charities with whom she worked. But publicly, she was seen to identify herself with victims – AIDS sufferers, the homeless, the oppressed and the victims of landmines. Deeply unhappy herself, she had hugged those in need and spoken with emotion about other people's suffering. She had touched people's hearts. Bogdanor argued that Diana's death helped people to define what they wanted the monarchy to be. Although the British were still a monarchical people, they wanted a demystified monarchy, in touch with their needs and prepared to address them. They wanted 'a practical monarchy'.

There is another, not necessarily conflicting suggestion: that the week's events showed a yearning for the ideal of monarchy. Monarchs used to have a vital, sacred role in society, but very few traces of this survive in modern Britain. Rowan Williams, the Anglican Archbishop of Wales, points out that in the secular society we have become there is no easy way back for the monarch to represent the sacred, the unquestioned 'given' in human affairs.

Diana's death produced an unexpected outpouring of egalitarian rituals. People demanded that the Queen and other members of the royal family participate in these rituals. 'She must be with us. She must share our grief. She must show us hers.' Perhaps, as Rowan Williams argues, what we saw was 'a potent lament for a lost sacredness, magical and highly personal, but equally a ritualized focus for public loyalty. The lost icon was not simply the dead princess; it was a whole mythology of social cohesion around anointed authority and mystery – ambiguous, not very articulate and not easy for either right or left in simple political terms.'

As the public expressions of grief subsided, it is also important to note that whatever accusations were made by newspapers and those grieving in the streets, there was another point of view. The Queen received thousands of letters from ordinary people all over the country. Many said something to the effect that they had 'never written before to a public figure, let alone to the Queen', but they felt that they must express their sympathy and outrage for the way in which she had been attacked by the press. 'We do not feel like this,' they said. Altogether, it seems clear to me that the week was an affirmation of the vital importance of the Queen in the life of the nation.

A few weeks later, in November, at an official luncheon to celebrate her Golden Wedding anniversary, the Queen acknowledged that the monarchy is a living thing that must always change. She said that, like the government, the monarchy 'exists only with the support and consent of the people'. Consent to politicians is expressed through the ballot box. 'For us, a royal family, however, the message is often harder to read, obscured as it can be by deference, rhetoric or the conflicting currents of public opinion. But read it we must.' She thanked people for their support during the troubled days after Diana's death, and went on to say,

'It is you, if I may now speak to all of you directly, who have seen us through, and helped us to make our duty fun. We are deeply grateful to you, each and every one.' Then she went on to talk about her husband of 50 years. 'He is someone who doesn't take easily to compliments,' she said. 'But he has, quite simply, been my strength and stay all these years, and I and his whole family, in this and many other countries, owe him a debt greater than he would ever claim or we shall ever know.'

For his part, Tony Blair used the occasion to affirm his monarchist credentials, calling the Queen 'a symbol of unity in a world of insecurity where nothing stays the same'. He said, like all prime ministers before him, how much he valued his weekly meetings with the Queen. 'There are only two people in the world, frankly, to whom a prime minister can say what he likes about his Cabinet colleagues. One's the wife, the other's the Queen.' Her advice was worth having not just because of her experience, but because 'she is an extraordinarily shrewd and perceptive observer of the world'.

He spoke also of the misconceptions that accompanied 'the terrible test' of the Princess's death. 'I know, too, contrary to some of the hurtful things that were said at the time, how moved you were by the outpouring of grief which followed. You sought, at all times, as a family to help and do the best by the boys, and that is the way it should have been and was.'

He said that 'a strong and flourishing monarchy can play the same full part in a new modern Britain as it has in the past… My generation pays tribute to you today with every bit as much force as older generations do. For you stand as our Queen for those values of duty and service that are timeless.' He ended by saying, 'You, Ma'am, are a symbol of unity in a world of insecurity… You are our Queen. We respect and cherish you. You are, simply, the Best of British.'

But Blair's relationship with the royal family was not quite so straightforward. Most of his Cabinet and many of those around him were said to be republican, including his wife, Cherie. In his first administration Blair carried out the most radical series of constitutional reforms seen in Britain since the Great Reform Act of 1832. He incorporated the European Social Chapter, passed a Human Rights Act, removed all but 92 hereditary peers from the House of Lords,

In November 1997, the Queen and Prince Philip celebrated their golden wedding anniversary with a service of thanksgiving in Westminster Abbey.

established a directly elected mayor in London and pursued devolution for the non-English parts of the United Kingdom.

The Queen still sets great store by the fact that she was crowned Queen of the United Kingdom and Northern Ireland, and devolution clearly concerns her. Scotland has now been given a directly elected Parliament and Wales a National Assembly. The Queen opened both. She told one member of her family recently that it was still too early to say what the impact will be.

The family has made a concerted effort to show that Scotland means more than being just the location of its holiday home, Balmoral. Princess Anne has become more active north of the border, where she is a popular figure. Prince William's decision to go to St Andrews University has been well received locally and boosted applications to study there.

In her Christmas speech of 1997, the Queen made clear her belief in the benefit of the union. 'Recent developments at home, which have allowed Scotland and Wales greater say in the way they are governed, should be seen in that light and as proof that the kingdom can still enjoy all the benefits of remaining united. Being united – that is, feeling a unity of purpose – is the glue that binds together the members of a family, a country, a Commonwealth. Without it, the parts are only fragments of a whole; with it, we can be much more than the sum of those fragments.'

The question of unity took another form in Australia. By the end of the millennium, the passion with which the Queen had been greeted there in 1954 was gone, if not quite forgotten. As Australia had developed into a regional power, with a growing Asian population, its links to Britain had inevitably diminished. A republican movement had grown in strength. In November 1999, Australians voted in a fiercely fought referendum as to whether they should retain the Queen as head of state. Many expected the republican cause to win – but nearly 55 per cent of the population voted in favour of the monarchy.

Four months later, the Queen flew to Australia for her thirteenth tour since she arrived on *Gothic* for her first triumphal visit. She addressed the issue directly, saying: 'I have always made it clear that the future of the monarchy in Australia is an issue for you, the Australian people, and you alone to decide by democratic and constitutional means. It should not be otherwise.' She spoke of her pleasure at being their Queen and of her long personal attachment to the country, saying, 'Whatever the future may bring, my lasting respect and deep affection for Australia and Australians everywhere will remain as strong as ever. That is what I have come here to say. That is why I am pleased to be back.'

The Times wrote of the tour, 'The Queen's impressive display of statesmanship charmed republican and monarchist alike.'

Tony Blair was the first of the Queen's prime ministers who was not even born when she came to the throne in 1952.

At home she continued to try to adapt to the demands of the times. Palace expenses were cut back substantially, thanks to the reforms begun in the mid-1980s and continued since. The cost of the monarchy to the taxpayer was reduced by 55 per cent during the 1990s, to £37 million. The costs of the presidency in many republics is far higher.

But the decade had taken a toll. The Queen no longer headed the model family created in the era of Victoria. Magic and mystery had been lost in the tawdry sadness of divorces and the spiteful way in which the press often covered the family's problems. Many journalists seemed to believe that they had a right, if not a duty, to be more aggressive about members of the royal family than any other individuals.

At the beginning of the new millennium, the republican tendency in the Blair government was reflected in much of the media. But the media did not reflect the views of most of the population. The monarchy, and the Queen in particular, still had the overwhelming support of the people – as it had since the start of her reign.

nine

Fifty Years On

Just months before Princess Elizabeth's accession, Britain presented an illustration of itself to the world. The Festival of Britain was staged in 1951 with the King and the Queen as patrons. Clement Attlee was Prime Minister, and the Labour government supported the festival, which was four years in the making. Its centrepiece was a celebratory exhibition on the South Bank in London. The festival was both a prayer for the future and a tribute the country paid itself for having defeated Nazism and for remaining a bastion of freedom. It also marked the centenary of the Great Exhibition, masterminded by Prince Albert.

The official handbook reads today like a guide to a lost planet. Its self-proclaimed intention was to display British achievements in 'one united act of national reassessment and one corporate reaffirmation of faith in the nation's future'. It was far from dispassionate; its proud purpose was to demonstrate Britain's 'contributions to civilization'. It extolled both the land and the people of Britain.

The British were described as 'one of the most-mixed people in the world', the result of a series of invasions by, among others, the Celts, the Romans and the Anglo-Saxons. Then, 'less than two hundred years after the Anglo-Saxons had settled in, St Augustine's mission brought a new infusion of Christianity to Britain'. The land and the people then accommodated and absorbed both Viking and Norman invaders.

Although the ancient dead were buried, 'it is the very blood they brought here that runs in us – yet, whether they came as conquerors or men of peace, all of them suffered a sea change on the way. They were absorbed into the life that was here before them, and themselves became islanders of a land that moulded

◁ King George VI and Queen Elizabeth at the opening of the 1951 Festival of Britain.

the thoughts, the feelings, the behaviour of them all into a whole which is our British way of life and our tradition.'

But what clues were there to British 'native genius'? They were displayed in a pavilion called 'The Lion and the Unicorn'. These symbolized 'two of the main qualities of the national character: on the one hand, realism and strength, on the other fantasy, independence and imagination'. There was also pride in the fact that the English language now united 250 million people around the world. 'The English Bible is still the great beacon for the language. Into successive versions of that Bible went the pride of English penmanship and the pick of English words: out of it came a resonance and radiance which have suffused all our later literature and speech.' And then, of course, came Shakespeare, 'who took the language in his hand and made words do things that had never been dreamed of and enshrined his mother-tongue in monumental plays'. Chaucer and T.S. Eliot were honoured, as were Defoe, Swift, Sterne, Carlyle, Dickens, Lewis Carroll, Gainsborough and Constable.

How else could 'an exhibition of tangible things…throw more light on the varieties of the national character?' The British had 'a continuing impulse to develop and enlarge, whenever opportunity offered, certain kinds of freedom – particularly freedom of worship, freedom of government, and personal freedom'. The examples given were Magna Carta, the House of Commons' struggle with Charles I, Milton's 1644 pamphlet 'Areopagitica' ('a spearhead for the breakthrough into freedom of the press'), freedom for Catholic worship, freedom for labour, and the suffragettes.

If any overseas visitor were still none the wiser about the British national character, 'it might console him to know that the British people are themselves still very much in the dark about it. For them, the British character is as easy to identify, and as difficult to define, as a British nonsense rhyme:

> The lion and unicorn
> Were fighting for the crown;
> The lion beat the unicorn
> All around the town,

Some gave them white bread
And some gave them brown;
Some gave them plum cake
And sent them out of town.'

Fifty years later, another Labour government staged a show on the banks of the Thames. The Millennium Dome was built on the occasion of the two thousandth anniversary of the birth of Christ, and was supposed to symbolize Britain in the same way that the Festival of Britain had done. But the exhibition barely mentioned Christianity and it symbolized little that was great about Britain at the turn of the millennium.

The £800 million construction was conceived by politicians and surrounded by management discord. The product of compromises by committees, its content was at best jolly and at worst vacuous. The exhibitions were dominated by the stamps of their commercial sponsors rather than by any enduring message.

The Millennium Dome, on the banks of the River Thames in Greenwich, was intended to be an attractive display of the best of Britain at the beginning of the twenty-first century. It failed.

One of the main attractions was a walk through an androgynous human body. Fast-food outlets seemed to be the principal shrines. Few of those Britons the government had insisted would flock to the show actually did so.

As a concession, the organizers agreed to allow a few minutes before the actual opening celebrations on New Year's Eve 2000 for the Archbishop of Canterbury, George Carey, to read prayers. He tried to remind people that this moment was supposed to celebrate the birth of Christ 2,000 years ago. Dr Carey later said it was one of the most mortifying experiences of his life. Surrounded by hostile drunks, the organizers were impatient to get him out of the way so the real, secular celebrations could begin in front of an invited audience, which included the Queen and Prince Philip, who sang 'Auld Lang Syne' with Mr and Mrs Blair.

The 1951 festival reflected historical pride, patriotism, religious conviction and a confident vision. Half a century later at the Dome, few of these qualities were in evidence.

The 50 years since the Queen's coronation have brought many benefits. Britain is more prosperous than at any previous time in its history. More people have more opportunities for individual happiness than ever. Many of the taboos and social stigmas that existed in the 1950s are gone. Women have far more power and freedom than before. Society is fluid and in many ways more tolerant. To take just one example, homosexuality was illegal in 1952 – now homosexuals form a strong political lobby, and there have been openly gay members of the Cabinet. We have become a more open, racially mixed country; immigrants and their descendants make up some 7 per cent of the population. Society is much more diverse, especially in London, which is a cosmopolitan city. Dress is more varied and casual, and the choice of foods is far greater than before.

In the last 50 years, Britain has seen its role in the world shrink and has undergone constant social and economic upheaval. We have managed the extraordinary transition from a homogeneous, structured imperial power to a much more individualistic, heterogeneous member of the European Union without serious civil unrest. Our armed forces are far smaller than in 1952, but

Britain still has one of the world's best militaries, as we showed in the Gulf War and more recently in Kosovo, Sierra Leone and Afghanistan.

The divisions that dominated British life in 1952 are much less rigid. Wealth has been spread between classes, particularly in the last 20 years. There is much better housing. Educational opportunities have widened; tertiary education was the privilege of the few in the 1950s – now it is within the reach of almost all. Politicians have hailed the advent of a 'classless society', and class distinctions are certainly far less rigid than they were half a century ago. Prosperity and mobility have brought new opportunities.

But there is a downside. The appearance of our cities and much of the countryside has been completely changed, often for the worse. Motorways have been cut harshly through beautiful areas; the hearts of many towns have been destroyed by insensitive developers, bad architects and careless planners. The regions of Britain have lost much of their traditional identities and there is far less strength in local communities. Suburbanization has spread; the pull of London has been relentless. The north is still poorer than the south of the country and suffers serious racial disharmony despite the ideal of 'multi-culturalism'. Successive governments have failed to solve the intractable problems of our public services.

Education may be more widely available, but it is shallower; history is ignored as never before. In the early 1950s people's sexual behaviour was often unhappily restricted; now there appear to be almost no restraints. Popular culture has made us more insensitive. Films, books, tabloid newspapers, music and computer games have all become more gory and explicit; reticence and discretion are now made to appear unusual. Tolerance has led to irresponsibility; Britain has the highest rate of teenage pregnancies in Europe. The easy access to drugs threatens the lives of young people.

At the beginning of the twenty-first century many of the habits and beliefs that previously held society together have disappeared. Christian congregations have diminished sharply – indeed in 2001, the leader of the Catholic Church in England and Wales declared that Christianity had been 'vanquished' in Britain. Respect for institutions has declined, and with it the standing of the entire political class. Politicians are unable to inspire crowds with their visions;

instead they dispense sound bites fitted to focus groups. In the 2001 election the turn-out was one of the lowest ever. Governments face new problems – an underclass that is hard to reach, a rise in violent crimes and other offences, family breakdown and what sometimes seems to be a moral vacuum. Tony Blair said in 1995, 'We enjoy a thousand material advantages over any previous generation and yet we suffer a depth of insecurity and spiritual doubt they never knew.'

The new generation takes for granted the sweeping social and sexual changes that disconcert many of their parents. They have, on the whole, less sense of history; for them the Empire has no meaning except perhaps a vague feeling of guilt imparted to them at school. They pay little attention to the Queen or to

Prince Charles celebrating the twenty-first anniversary of the Prince's Trust with the Spice Girls.

state events. Many of them do not know the words of the national anthem. It is extraordinary to think that only 40 years ago 'God Save the Queen' was played every night in cinemas and theatres across the land. Unlike in the United States, patriotism is shunned.

British society is more complicated than before. New distinctions and new orthodoxies have replaced the old. In 1952, there were more class divisions but there was also greater courtesy. Today, those who are uneasy at the pace of social change are often derided. Public service, tradition and authority were respected far more 50 years ago than now. Indeed, they used to be inculcated in schools. One young woman recently said to me, when considering the Queen's devotion to duty, 'For my generation, duty is rather a sad idea.'

National unity has declined both constitutionally and culturally. The increasing integration of the European Union has caused Parliament to transfer aspects of Britain's sovereignty to European institutions. The Queen's kingdom has been utterly transformed and in some senses diminished since 1952.

In all the turmoil and change, only the Queen has remained the same – a still small voice of calm at the vortex of the storm.

There is an unhappy history amongst our intellectual elite of failing to take pride in our heritage. George Orwell identified this in his 1941 essay 'The Lion and the Unicorn': 'England is perhaps the only great country whose intellectuals are ashamed of their own nationality. In left-wing circles it is always felt that there is something slightly disgraceful in being an Englishman and that it is a duty to snigger at every institution, from horse racing to suet puddings. It is a strange fact, but it is unquestionably true, that almost any English intellectual would feel more ashamed of standing to attention during "God Save the King" than of stealing from the poorbox.'

Sometimes it is necessary to counter that tendency head on. I think that Britain has been enormously fortunate in having for 50 years a head of state who has performed her job with the devotion, honour, discretion and constancy of the Queen. The debt she is owed is incalculable but huge.

Her roles as head of the armed forces and of the Church have become less significant to the country at large (though not to her) as those two traditional pillars of the monarchy have weakened. But her role as head of the nation has survived. That is largely because of her own personality and record.

The Queen has not sat back and let the tide of events surge over her. She has responded to the demand for greater openness in ways unthinkable in previous reigns. George V warned his son Edward VIII not to get too close to his subjects: 'Always remember who you are,' he said. Distance was then part of the system. The Queen has had to make herself more accessible – and yet still be apart.

She has shared far more of her thoughts with her people than any of her predecessors. In her 1992 speech at the Guildhall, she talked frankly of her woes. In her Christmas broadcast that same year she said, 'The prayers, understanding and sympathy given to us by so many of you, in good times and bad, have lent us great support and encouragement. It has touched me deeply that much of this has come from those of you who have troubles of your own.'

Yet somehow she has managed to maintain the mystique of monarchy. In July 2001 I talked to guests at a garden party at Buckingham Palace. They included doctors, charity workers, local officials, policemen – all were delighted to be there and those who had talked to the Queen were beaming. They spoke of the interest she showed in them through her questions, and praised the quiet, unpretentious way in which she symbolized the country.

As one of her former private secretaries said to me, 'Through the quarter century I worked at the Palace I saw nobody who failed to be moved on meeting her. There's always something very special about meeting her face to face, and there is undoubtedly an element of romance, which is very important.'

Her early, benign critic, John Grigg said, 'Even though people don't go round throwing their hats in the air and saying how marvellous she is, I think they feel it – because that sort of steadiness in the times that we've lived through has been really precious.'

Douglas Hurd, the former Foreign Secretary, said to me, 'Her success has been to keep her nerve, keep her character, keep the essential dignity of her position going in 50 years when nerve and character and dignity have been rather at a discount and all kinds of destructive waves have swept across the world, including her own people and to some extent her own family.' The historian Sir Maurice Shock made a different point: 'Her genius has been to preside over literally revolutionary changes in the country over almost half a century and never be seen to be partisan, yet always to be in control. It is because we have no idea what she thinks that she has succeeded.'

The Queen has allowed the monarchy to evolve, but she has not pandered to the mood swings of time. She is realistic about change. Her deliberate, cautious behaviour may seem fuddy-duddy to some, but it appears eminently reassuring to most. She understands that for the monarchy it is not ephemeral popularity that matters, it is long-term consent.

She has faced down the turmoil of her reign through strength of character. She is steadfast, her own person, not easily swayed. She tries not to be in the front of what's taking place, but not to be left too far behind. She seems to have imbibed at birth the spirit of Rudyard Kipling's 'If':

> If you can keep your head when all about you
> Are losing theirs and blaming it on you.

In June 1994 it was remarkable and moving to see the Queen on the beach at Arromanches, celebrating the fiftieth anniversary of D-Day. She was clearly happy as the veterans – her generation – marched past. There was a rare catch in her voice as she and the old men revelled in their pride in each other. Her heir, Prince Charles, also there, was equally moved.

The following year, on the fiftieth anniversary of VE Day, I was amongst the vast crowds who stood outside Buckingham Palace. On the balcony were the same three women who had stood there in 1945 – the Queen Mother, the Queen and Princess Margaret. It was an extraordinary moment, one that symbolized all the strengths of this Queen – history, continuity, courage and leadership.

A unique symbol of unity at home, she has been an extraordinary ambassador abroad. She has known every US president since Truman, who was only one of the first of hundreds of foreign leaders to be captivated by her. Former President Bill Clinton told me that when he was in Britain as a student in the

1960s, 'I thought she and Prince Philip seemed elegant and stoic.' When, as President, he got to know her, he found her 'open, candid and warm'. He spent the night before the D-Day commemoration with her aboard *Britannia*. 'She loves her country and loves its history. She has done everything she possibly could to elevate her role in the best sense, but to still show a common touch, a sense of being in tune with the people. She has done her duty. Life thrust her into certain circumstances and she did an excellent job of dealing with the hand she was dealt. We should all do so well.'

When people speak of 'the Queen' in other countries, they are not referring to the Queen of Thailand or the Queen of the Netherlands, however admirable they may be. They are talking of Elizabeth II. One reason for her international reach is the Commonwealth, which she has nurtured so well and which now has 54 members. It makes Britain's the only international monarchy and the Queen a world figure.

Kofi Annan, the Secretary General of the United Nations, says that, 'She is the one person all Commonwealth leaders look up to and look forward to seeing. Her leadership of the group has been remarkable. Everyone is touched by her knowledge, her sensitivity and her incredible humour. You know you are dealing with someone who understands the world and who has a calmness and serenity that are very impressive.'

In 1996, Vaclav Havel, the President of the Czech Republic, praised the Queen at the end of her successful visit to his country for combining the 'dignity of the throne' with 'an open, honest attitude, an ability to take things as they are, and a sense of humour. It was not just her upbringing, experience and sense of perspective,' he said. 'It goes beyond this to the real personal charisma of someone who has found the proper measure of playing the part.'

When the Queen came to the throne in 1952, Czechoslovakia was descending into the long, brutal night of Stalinism. By the 1990s, it had finally emerged – and the Queen was still on the throne. Such continuity is treasured in a place like Prague, where the communists tried to destroy all history. Havel, and the tens of thousands of Czechs who lined the streets to see the Queen, were far more interested in her and the institution she represents than in the travails of her family.

The Queen and Prince Philip amongst the war graves in Normandy during the D-Day celebrations in June 1994.

On the fiftieth anniversary of VE Day, the same three women stood on the balcony of Buckingham Palace as had stood there in 1945. Huge crowds cheered this moving sight.

Prince Charles, the Queen, the UN Secretary General Kofi Annan and Prime Minister Tony Blair outside Westminster Abbey before the Observance of Commonwealth Service in March 2000.

(Havel was also delighted when his dog, a large beast, instantly identified the Queen as a dog person; she was happy too.)

At home she has been a support to all her prime ministers; not one of them has had anything but praise for her role. Tony Blair came to office wary of the monarchy's formality; he too has come to respect and value her. Publicly, she embodies self-sacrifice and individual effort. Princess Diana brilliantly personified the importance of charity work, but that has always been integral to the life of the Queen. Through its increasing attention to the voluntary sector, the royal family has adapted its traditional role to provide a focus for unity. The monarch will always attract a much wider constituency than any politician.

Since Princess Diana's death, and the turmoil that surrounded it, the Queen's role has subtly changed. Buckingham Palace is said to be 'listening' more, taking more soundings to keep in touch better with the general public. The Queen's diary has been altered. Even before Diana's death, the Palace had undertaken a comprehensive review of the Queen's engagements to ensure that she met a wider spectrum of her people. 'Theme days' were started, in which she meets workers in the private sector, instead of the more typical visits to the public sector. Such days have included visits to the City of London, the theatre world, the publishing and broadcasting industries.

In September 2001, she was quick to react to the terrorist attacks upon New York and Washington. Americans were touched when she ordered the Guard at

The Queen was visibly moved at a memorial service for the victims of the 11 September terrorist attacks in America. 'Grief is the price we pay for love,' she later said.

Buckingham Palace to play 'The Star-Spangled Banner'. At the service in St Paul's Cathedral to commemorate those murdered, she personified the anguish that was so widely felt; wiping her tears, she showed her emotion unusually clearly. She had a private sorrow as well: her best friend, Lord Carnarvon, had died suddenly on 11 September.

She then wrote a letter that was read out during a ceremony at St Thomas's Church in New York for the families of the British victims of the terrorist attacks. In it, she judged the moment perfectly, ending with the memorable phrase: 'Grief is the price we pay for love.' Bill Clinton, who was in the congregation, said, 'It was a stunning sentence, so wise and so true. It somehow made people feel better, making us understand that we were grieving because we had that love.'

Sometimes it seems hard to see how the monarchy can survive in today's secular, cynical age. But it has outlived worse periods in the past. In the latter years of the nineteenth century, the monarchy was first put at risk and then saved by Queen Victoria. Her immediate predecessors – George III, George IV and William IV – had been described in turn as an imbecile, a profligate and a buffoon. Earlier in her reign, Victoria, acting on the crucial advice of Prince

Albert, who insisted that monarchy be above party, began to define the limits and establish the success of constitutional monarchy. But after Prince Albert's death, Queen Victoria became known as the reclusive Widow of Windsor. There was resentment that she was paid but did almost no work. She was lampooned and abused; republicanism flourished, so much so that in 1870, after the abdication of Napoleon III, 'La Marseillaise' was sung in Trafalgar Square.

The constitutional writer Walter Bagehot warned that Victoria was damaging the monarchy. 'To be invisible is to be forgotten,' he wrote. 'To be a symbol and an effective symbol, you must be vividly and often seen.' In 1876 Victoria re-emerged and became a strong and increasingly popular monarch. The years after 1876 were her most successful; her Golden Jubilee in 1887 was a triumph.

The Victorian monarchy rested both on Empire and on the notion of the ideal middle-class family. The imperial model lasted until the end of George VI's reign. The 'family monarchy' survived until the end of the 1980s. It was destroyed not just by the failed marriages of younger royals, but also by unending, sometimes vindictive and often politically motivated media scrutiny.

It is the triumph of this Queen that, despite the media criticisms, she has maintained an emotional focus through all the extraordinary political and social change. She was needed at Dunblane in 1996 just as much as at Aberfan in 1967. Her stoic presence has been the centre that held. She has been able, in the words of Vernon Bogdanor, 'to interpret the nation to itself'.

There is a choice. Prince Philip himself has said, 'If the people of this country want a republic, that's a perfectly sensible alternative.' So far, thanks to this Queen, the overwhelming majority of people still prefer the monarchy. I quoted Harold Macmillan talking with horror of the political nonentities who would become presidents in a republic. Some would be better than that. But in a republican system we would inevitably have as president a politician promoted for party reasons. We would never again have someone who would be able, as the Queen has been able, to personify and unify the country, beyond the political coil.

The jewel of the British constitution is the Crown. John Grigg speaks of 'the genius of constitutional monarchy'. The philosopher Roger Scruton describes it as 'the light above politics, which shines down on the human bustle from a calmer and more exalted sphere. Not being elected by popular vote, the monarch cannot be understood as representing the interest only of the present generation. He or she is born into the position, and also passes it on to a legally defined successor. The monarch is in a real sense the voice of history.'

David Owen says, 'If you've got a monarchy and particularly a monarchy that has done as well as this one, you don't change it for something else which shows no sign of being better and a good many signs of being a good deal worse. As long as the Queen's heirs and successors conduct themselves well, I think we'll go on with the monarchy. But if we have a bad egg, somebody who fouls it up, then the mood of the country could change very quickly indeed.'

When the time comes, there is every reason to think that Prince Charles will become a fine king. It is a task for which he has been preparing all his life. The job of Prince of Wales is almost more difficult than that of monarch, but he has created a valuable role for himself. As well as founding and sustaining the Prince's Trust, he has courageously defended fine architecture, and made seminal contributions to the debates on the environment and comparative religion. He has also articulated well the concerns of many sections of society about the nature and direction of change. When he becomes king, he will do the job differently but he will do it well.

A more difficult question is whether it is fair to ask Prince William to surrender his life to this particular constitutional system in a country that may no longer be emotionally capable of supporting it. But that is a decision for the future. For the present it is enough to recognize the extraordinary reign of the Queen. As her late Private Secretary Martin Charteris used to say, 'May the Queen live for ever.'

In the end the survival of the monarchy depends on the importance that people accord to history, to emotion and belief as well as to reason in public life. The republican view is, in essence, that you cannot have a 'modern' society if you have at its core an element that depends on belief not reason. In my view, that is completely untrue. Britain has 'modernized' throughout the last 50 years. You can be both mature and modern and still have icons, as Vaclav Havel said.

The historian Elizabeth Longford argues that the monarchy 'has been with the nation, for better and for worse, for a thousand years; and though such a period in the sight of eternity is "but as yesterday" in human terms, this long span brings a sense of timelessness that stirs the heart and imagination'. It can also be the object of love, for it is not 'quite rational, not wholly logical, nor even fully intelligible to itself or to us [so] it can become the national focus for service and chivalry as well as fantasy and dreams'.

It is hard for any magic, mystery, fantasy or dreams to survive in a world of new media, new demands for 'accountability', new hypocrisies that question every last penny the Queen spends, every move she makes and every word she utters. On the other hand, as John Wells, the historian and satirist, once said to me, 'Monarchy represents the mystical idea that there is a coherent centre to things. In recent years we've stolen the lead off the roof, the windows have been broken, people are almost urinating on the altar. But the funny thing in all systems of belief, including monarchy, is that just at the moment when the shrine has been smashed and the altar broken, the pendulum swings and there is a popular reaction to defend it.' I think that will happen for the Queen, during this Golden Jubilee and beyond.

The Queen represents the values that many ordinary people feel, even if they are not always acclaimed nowadays. She needs and is touched by the personal reassurances that she gets from her people – the letters, gifts and the smiles she receives when she stops and talks to the crowds that turn out to see her. One woman close to her says, 'I felt that so many of those people who wrote to her after the Princess was killed and at other times were saying (literally), "*Thank God* there is someone like you who stands up for the core values we know in our hearts to be right – but it takes much courage these days to put your head above the parapet and risk having the mob pelt you with screaming insults. Thank you for doing so."'

Her Christmas broadcast of 2000 was from the heart of our mysterious monarch, and it revealed more clearly than usual why she is loved. She said that the birth of Jesus was 'the true millennium anniversary'. She thought that the impact of Christ's life was all around us, and the true measure of his influence was 'in the good works quietly done by millions of men and women day in and day out through the centuries'.

She paid tribute to the divine inspiration of other religions and went on, 'To many of us, our beliefs are of fundamental importance. For me the teachings of

The Queen Mother embodies the past, the Queen the present, and Prince William the future; the strength of the monarchy is continuity.

in which I try to live my life. I, like so many of you, have drawn great comfort in difficult times from Christ's words and example. I believe that the Christian message, in the words of a familiar blessing, remains profoundly important to us all:

> Go forth into the world in peace,
> be of good courage,
> hold fast that which is good,
> render to no man evil for evil,
> strengthen the faint hearted,
> support the weak,
> help the afflicted,
> honour all men.

It is a simple message of compassion – and yet as powerful today as ever, 2,000 years after Christ's birth.'

The Queen's heartfelt words elicited hundreds of letters of praise and thanks from her listeners around the country. Her personal commitment to faith, hope and charity was made by a woman who has kept every one of the solemn vows she made to God and her people 50 years ago. It is an extraordinary achievement, which should be celebrated, honoured and cherished.

Acknowledgements

The story of the Queen has been often covered. I owe great gratitude to those who have done it before me, usually at greater length and with greater erudition. In particular, I wish to thank the following authors, whose works I have drawn upon:

Ronald Allison and Sarah Riddell (eds.), *The Royal Encyclopaedia* (Macmillan 1991);
Vernon Bogdanor, *The Monarchy and the Constitution* (Clarendon Press 1995);
Sarah Bradford, *Elizabeth* (Heinemann 1996);
Kenneth Harris, *The Queen* (Weidenfeld & Nicolson 1994);
John Hartley, *Accession* (Quartet 1992);
Anthony Jay, *Elizabeth R* (BBC 1992);
Elizabeth Longford, *Elizabeth R* (Weidenfeld & Nicolson 1983);
Ben Pimlott, *The Queen* (HarperCollins 1996);
Frank Prochaska, *Royal Bounty* (Allen Lane 1995);
Kenneth Rose, *Kings, Queens and Courtiers* (Weidenfeld & Nicolson 1985).

Many people who have worked for the Queen in different capacities, or have known her as a friend, have talked to me and helped me. I am grateful to them all, as well as to those who gave interviews for the accompanying television series whom I quote in this book. My thanks are also due to both Kenneth Rose and Vernon Bogdanor, who were kind enough to read parts of the manuscript and point out my mistakes.

I would like to thank George Carey and John Bridcut of Mentorn Barraclough Carey, who skilfully produced and directed the series. I was helped especially by Anna Murphy, the assistant producer and a researcher whose insights and industry were invaluable to both the films and this book. Helena Bullivant was an exemplary production manager.

At the BBC I thank Lorraine Heggessey, Controller of BBC 1, for her support, and Richard Klein, Senior Commissioning Editor; at BBC Books, Sally Potter, who commissioned the book, Susannah Parker, the picture researcher, and Martin Redfern, whose style, judgement and hard work as editor helped me enormously. At Simon and Schuster in New York I thank, as always, my magnificent editor, Alice Mayhew.

Index